D1568894

The Establishment of the State of Israel

MILESTONES IN MODERN WORLD HISTORY

600 · · · 1750 · · · 1940 · · · 2000

The Boer War

The Bolshevik Revolution

The British Industrial Revolution

The Chinese Cultural Revolution

The Collapse of the Soviet Union

The Congress of Vienna

The Cuban Revolution

D-Day and the Liberation of France

The End of Apartheid in South Africa

The Establishment of the State of Israel

The French Revolution and the Rise of Napoleon

The Great Irish Famine

The Indian Independence Act of 1947

The Iranian Revolution

The Manhattan Project

The Marshall Plan

The Mexican Revolution

The Treaty of Nanking

The Treaty of Versailles

The Universal Declaration of Human Rights

MILESTONES
IN MODERN
WORLD HISTORY

The Establishment of the State of Israel

LOUISE CHIPLEY SLAVICEK

CHELSEA HOUSE
An Infobase Learning Company

The Establishment of the State of Israel

Copyright © 2012 by Infobase Learning

Chelsea House
An imprint of Infobase Learning
132 West 31st Street
New York, NY 10001

Library of Congress Cataloging-in-Publication Data

Slavicek, Louise Chipley, 1956–
The establishment of the state of israel / by Louise Chipley Slavicek.
    p.   cm. — (Milestones in modern world history)
Includes bibliographical references and index.
ISBN 978-1-60413-917-4 (hardcover)
1. Jews—History—Juvenile literature. 2. Zionism—History—Juvenile literature. 3. Israel—History—Juvenile literature. I. Title. II. Series.
  DS118.S58 2011
  956.74'04—dc22   2011011609

Chelsea House books are available at special discounts when purchased in bulk quantities for businesses, associations, institutions, or sales promotions. Please call our Special Sales Department in New York at (212) 967-8800 or (800) 322-8755.

You can find Chelsea House on the World Wide Web at http://www.infobaselearning.com.

Text design by Erik Lindstrom
Cover design by Alicia Post
Composition by Keith Trego
Cover printed by Bang Printing, Brainerd, Minn.
Book printed and bound by Bang Printing, Brainerd, Minn.
Date printed: October 2011
Printed in the United States of America

10 9 8 7 6 5 4 3 2 1

This book is printed on acid-free paper.

CONTENTS

May 14, 1948

The State of Israel was born on a hot and humid May afternoon in 1948 in Tel Aviv, on the eastern coast of what was then called Palestine, a narrow strip of land bordered by the Mediterranean Sea, Egypt, Jordan, Syria, and Lebanon. The new Jewish state's birth took place 2,000 years after Palestine's Roman conquerors had exiled the Jews from the land once known as the Kingdom of Israel, and 28 years after Great Britain received an international mandate (or protectorship) to govern Palestine following World War I (1914–1918).

THE HOPE

The modest ceremony that marked the State of Israel's founding on May 14, 1948, was held in the Tel Aviv Museum of Art before an audience of 250 dignitaries—the largest number of people that could squeeze into the museum's main hall. Space was so tight in the building that the Palestinian Philharmonic Orchestra (soon to be renamed the Israel Philharmonic) was relegated to a second-floor balcony above the auditorium. At precisely 4:00 P.M., David Ben-Gurion, the leader of the 600,000 Jewish inhabitants of what would technically remain the British mandate of Palestine until midnight, the moment at which the last British troops were scheduled to evacuate the region, opened the ceremony by giving a loud rap with his gavel. Moments later, the Philharmonic Orchestra began playing the popular Jewish hymn—and new Israeli national anthem—"HaTikvah," Hebrew for "The Hope."

As the anthem's somber strains drifted down from the balcony above, Ben-Gurion's audience sang about the enduring hope of Jews everywhere to reclaim their scriptural "Promised Land" ever since their ancestors had been driven out by the Romans and dispersed throughout the globe:

> Our hope is not yet lost
> The hope of two thousand years,
> To be a free people in our land
> The land of Zion and Jerusalem.[1]

Once the music ended, Ben-Gurion, standing beneath a portrait of Theodor Herzl (1860–1904), founder of the modern Zionist movement to create a national refuge for persecuted Jews—a sovereign state in their ancient Middle Eastern homeland—began to speak. His text was the just-completed Israeli Declaration of Independence. "*Eretz Yisrael*" (Hebrew for "the Land of Israel"), he declared, was the historic "birthplace of the Jewish people. Here their spiritual, religious, and political identity was shaped. Here they first attained to statehood, created cultural values of national and universal significance, and gave to the world the eternal Book of Books [the Hebrew Bible]." Over the millennia following their expulsion from Eretz

Yisrael, the Jews had "kept faith" with the land they believed God had pledged to them and their descendants, Ben-Gurion continued. Harassed and marginalized almost everywhere they settled, Jews "never ceased to pray and hope for their return" to Israel, and "for the restoration in it of their political freedom."[2]

Reviewing the major events of the past several decades in Jewish history, Ben-Gurion recalled the massive ingathering of Zionist settlers to Mandatory Palestine in recent years as well as the murder of 6 million Jews by the Nazis during World War II (1939–1945). He then linked the right of the Jewish people to establish their state to a resolution regarding Palestine's future made by the international peacekeeping organization, the United Nations, in November 1947. According to the UN resolution of 1947, because of increasingly violent Jewish–Arab friction in Palestine, the country should be partitioned into two self-governing states once the British mandate ended. Jews were to receive a little more than 50 percent of the territory of Palestine for their new state, and the Arab Palestinians, the region's single largest ethnic group for the past 1,000 years, just under 50 percent for theirs. Enthusiastically embraced by most Jews, the UN resolution was roundly condemned by Arab Palestinians and their Arab neighbors throughout the Middle East, who insisted that the Jewish immigrants were interlopers and it was unjust to turn over any part of Palestine to Jewish control.

Ben-Gurion concluded by proclaiming the founding of the new state and calling for Jews everywhere "to rally round" his fellow Israelis "in the task of immigration and upbuilding, and to stand by them in the great struggle for the realization of the age-old dream—the redemption of Israel."[3] With that, the audience leapt to their feet to applaud the official establishment of *Medinath Yisrael* (Hebrew for the "State of Israel"). "All were seized by ineffable joy, their faces irradiated," Ben-Gurion's assistant, Ze'eve Sharef, later recalled.[4] A few hours after the ceremony, however, Ben-Gurion confided in his diary that,

On May 14, 1948, David Ben-Gurion, who was to become Israel's first prime minister, reads the Israeli Declaration of Independence at the Museum of Art in Tel Aviv, during the ceremonial founding of the State of Israel.

at the moment of Medinath Yisrael's establishment, he was "a mourner among the celebrants."[5]

Ben-Gurion's somber mood on May 14, 1948, was understandable. Over the past six months, Israeli forces had fought successfully against disorganized and inadequately armed Arab Palestinian militias and volunteer fighters from neighboring Arab countries to retain control of the territories allocated to the Jews in the UN partition resolution. Now, however, the Israelis faced far more formidable opponents on the battlefield. Determined to crush the Jewish state at its birth, the regular armies of five neighboring Arab countries began assembling along Israel's borders within hours of Israel's establishment. The next morning, as the sun rose over the newborn state, Egyptian, Jordanian, Syrian, Iraqi, and Lebanese troops invaded, launching what the Israelis call their War of Independence and the Arab Palestinians, more than a half century later, still refer to as *al-Nakba*—Arabic for "The Disaster."

A Promised Land
Won and Lost

The relationship of the Jewish people with the sliver of land on the eastern Mediterranean coast that became the State of Israel began some 4,000 years ago. Many scholars believe that the Jews' ancestors, the Hebrews, left their home in Ur, near the Euphrates River in southern Mesopotamia (modern Iraq), in about 1800 B.C. The Hebrews' destination was Canaan, an ancient region between the Mediterranean and the River Jordan that roughly corresponds to present-day Israel, the Gaza Strip, and the West Bank.

According to the Book of Genesis, which is part of both Hebrew Scriptures and the Christian Bible, Abraham, the first of the biblical founding fathers, led the band of emigrants to Canaan. God had made a promise to Abraham about Canaan, the Bible reports. He would give "all the land of Canaan" to

Abraham and his Hebrew descendants and help them make it into a great nation.[1] In return for this "Promised Land," God expected the Hebrews to honor and obey him.

THE BIRTH OF THE KINGDOM OF ISRAEL

In 1800 B.C., the Hebrews' Promised Land was not an empty territory waiting only for Abraham and his people to possess it. A number of ethnic groups already inhabited the region. Consequently, when the Hebrews arrived, they were unable to claim "all the land of Canaan" as their own. Instead, they settled in one of Canaan's least populated areas, the rocky hill country to the east of its green coastal plains. In their new homeland, the Hebrews herded sheep and goats and may have farmed part-time as well.

According to Scripture, after the Hebrews had lived in central Canaan for about two centuries, a deadly famine struck. Threatened with starvation, they had no choice but to abandon their Promised Land. Now generally known as the Israelites, in honor of Abraham's grandson, Jacob, who was given the name Israel, the Hebrews migrated southward, settling in the North African kingdom of Egypt. It was a decision they would come to regret. While Egypt's supreme leaders, the pharaohs, treated the newcomers well at first, they eventually forced the Israelites into slavery.

The Israelites finally rebelled against their powerful oppressors in about 1200 B.C. The Book of Exodus, another part of the Hebrew Scriptures and the Christian Bible, reports that they fled back toward their Promised Land under the guidance of the great religious leader and prophet Moses, with the Egyptian army pounding on their heels. After the Israelites reached Mount Sinai in the vast desert separating Egypt from Canaan, one of the most significant moments in the development of Judaism occurred. According to Scripture, God formed a covenant with the Israelites by presenting Moses with the

Ten Commandments, their fundamental moral and spiritual obligations to him and to one another. The Israelites' acceptance of the Ten Commandments firmly established them as monotheists, or worshippers of just one god. (The Israelites' monotheism set them apart from their other contemporaries in the ancient Middle East, who were polytheists, or worshippers of many deities.) In the first two commandments, God tells his people: "I am the LORD your God, who brought you out of the land of Egypt, out of the house of slavery. You shall have no other gods before Me."[2]

In the biblical narrative, the Israelites wandered in the Sinai Desert for 40 years before making their way back to central Canaan. After they returned to their Promised Land, their fortunes took a dramatic turn for the better. Within a little more than a century, the Israelites had conquered or absorbed most of the region's other ethnic groups, excepting their chief military rivals, the seafaring Philistines. In about 1030 B.C., all of the 12 Israelite tribes agreed for the first time to unite under a single ruler, the warrior-farmer Saul. Saul's ascension to the throne launched a golden era in the history of ancient Israel known as the United Monarchy period (1030–931 B.C.). Under the rule of Saul's famous successor, King David, who reigned from 1010 to 970 B.C., Israel became a major power in the Middle East, defeating the militaristic Philistines and expanding its territory from the coast of the Mediterranean south to the Red Sea and north into modern-day Syria.

THE REIGN OF KING SOLOMON

The Kingdom of Israel continued to prosper and consolidate under David's autocratic son, Solomon. During his nearly 40-year reign, King Solomon ordered the construction of many magnificent buildings, most of them in Jerusalem, the southern city his father had chosen as the kingdom's capital and spiritual center after wresting it from the Jebusites, a Canaanite tribe. Solomon's crowning achievement was the construction of an

This mosaic of ceramic tiles at the Meroth Synagogue in Galilee, Israel, depicts King David of Israel with Goliath's armor. A great warrior, king, and poet, he reigned over Judah circa 1010–1003 B.C., and over the united Kingdom of Israel circa 1003–970 B.C.

elaborate place of worship in Jerusalem, known in Jewish history as the First Temple. According to the Bible, it took seven years and tens of thousands of laborers to complete this holiest of all Hebrew shrines.

INTERNAL DIVISIONS AND FOREIGN THREATS

The Kingdom of Israel reached its political and economic apogee during Solomon's reign. Shortly after Solomon's death in 931 B.C., the kingdom began to disintegrate. As long as the ironfisted ruler had lived, Israel had remained unified. But when Solomon's son, Rehoboam, succeeded him as king, long-simmering resentments between the kingdom's northern and southern halves erupted into armed clashes. According to the Bible, the northerners were particularly angered by Rehoboam's refusal to reduce the high taxes imposed by his father to fund his building projects, most of which were centered in Jerusalem and other southern towns. By 931 B.C., the Hebrews' Promised Land had split into two warring kingdoms. The larger northern kingdom kept the name Israel and took Samaria as its capital, while the mountainous southern kingdom adopted the name of Judah and retained Jerusalem as its seat of government.

Over the course of the next two centuries, the two squabbling kingdoms were weakened by a series of civil wars and foreign invasions. Finally, in 722 B.C., the northern kingdom ceased to exist altogether when the Assyrian Empire of central Mesopotamia overran Israel, killing or deporting all its inhabitants and bringing in different ethnic groups to replace them. After declaring Israel an imperial province, the Assyrians brought in Babylonians, Syrians, and peoples from other Middle Eastern lands they had conquered to settle in the devastated region.

With the demise of the northern kingdom, only the people of Judah were left to carry on the ancient Hebrew religion, laws, and culture. (Many scholars believe that the word "Jew" is derived from the Hebrew word *Yahadut*, meaning "man of

Judah.") In 586 B.C., less than 200 years after the fall of Israel, the Babylonians, an ancient people of southern Mesopotamia, conquered Judah. They demolished the great temple built by Solomon in Jerusalem and carried off 10,000 prominent Judahites to their capital city of Babylon, according to the

PSALM 137

One of the most poignant of the lyrical psalms (or poems) of the Hebrew Bible is the 137th Psalm, composed during the Babylonian Exile, when 10,000 Jews were taken to Babylon as captives following the conquest of Judah by the Babylonian army in 586 B.C. The psalm expresses the deep yearning of the new exiles to return home to Zion:

> By the rivers of Babylon,
> There we sat down and wept,
> When we remembered Zion.
> Upon the willows in the midst of it
> We hung our harps.
> For there our captors demanded of us songs,
> And our tormentors' mirth, saying,
> "Sing us one of the songs of Zion."
> How can we sing the LORD'S song
> In a foreign land?
> If I forget you, O Jerusalem,
> May my right hand forget her skill.
> May my tongue cleave to the roof of my mouth
> If I do not remember you,
> If I do not exalt Jerusalem
> Above my chief joy.*

* Psalms 137:1-6, New American Standard Bible.

After being held for years in captivity in Babylon, the exiled Jews were allowed to return to Israel, where they would rebuild Jerusalem, including their great temple, today known as the Second Temple.

Hebrew Scriptures. When Jerusalem fell to the Babylonian army, another large group of Jews fled Judah for northeastern Egypt. Like the Babylonian exiles, the Egyptian exiles faithfully maintained their Jewish identity and traditions.

JUDAH'S CHANGING FORTUNES

During the sixth century B.C., a new Middle Eastern super-power, Persia (modern Iran), conquered the Babylonians and claimed Judah for its own expanding empire. Shortly afterward, the Persian ruler, Cyrus the Great, permitted the Jewish exiles in Babylonia to return home. Under Persia's lenient rule, Judah's Jewish inhabitants were granted a significant degree of freedom in running their own affairs. They were also allowed to rebuild their great temple in Jerusalem. Known in Jewish history as the Second Temple, the building was dedicated in 515 B.C.

A little less than 200 years after Judah became a Persian province, the Macedonian warrior-king Alexander the Great conquered the Persian Empire, and Judah fell under the control of Macedonia and Greece. Like the Persians before them, Judah's new rulers allowed the Jews to practice their religion as they chose. That changed, however, after the Seleucids, a dynasty (ruling group) descended from one of Alexander's generals, took charge of Judah, now generally known as Judea, in 200 B.C. The second Seleucid king, Antiochus IV, was determined to make his Jewish subjects adopt Hellenistic (or Greek) culture. To the horror of the Judeans, he dedicated the Second Temple in Jerusalem to the worship of the chief Greek god, Zeus. When Antiochus followed up this outrage by ordering the Jews to renounce their religious beliefs on penalty of death, the Judeans rose up in rebellion.

Under the leadership of the priestly Hasmonean family, and particularly Judah Maccabee, the rebels eventually won back Jerusalem and reclaimed the Second Temple in 164 B.C. The beleaguered Seleucid dynasty officially remained in power in

Judea for another 25 years, but only because the Seleucid kings agreed to restore religious freedom to their Jewish subjects. In 141 B.C., under the skillful leadership of Simon Hasmonean, the Jews expelled the last of the Seleucid garrisons from Judea, clearing the way for total self-rule. The following year, the first independent Jewish state since the conquest of Judah by the Babylonians four centuries earlier was officially declared in Jerusalem, with Simon Hasmonean as the Jews' top political and religious leader.

After the Hasmonean family quickly established a heredi-tary monarchy, Judea flourished under their rule. By the end of the second century B.C., the Hasmonean state had expanded to include all the territories of the former Kingdom of Israel at the time of Solomon's reign. During the reign of the tyranni-cal Alexander Yannai (103–76 B.C.), however, the state began a downward slide. After his death, the kingdom was further weak-ened when Yannai's two sons battled each other for the throne.

ROMAN DOMINATION

In 63 B.C., the Roman general Pompey took advantage of the civil war raging in Judea to conquer the Hasmonean kingdom and annex it as a client state of the Roman Republic's rapidly expanding empire. Following the demise of the Hasmonean kingdom in the first century B.C., an independent Jewish state would not arise again in the Jews' biblical Promised Land for another 2,000 years.

At first, Roman rule in Judea was relatively lenient. Roman officials granted Judea's Jewish majority religious freedom and substantial political self-rule. Around 40 B.C., however, the Roman government strengthened its control over Judea by appointing Herod, a strongly pro-Roman con-vert to Judaism, as king. In A.D. 6, following Herod's death, the Romans tightened their control over Judea even further by placing the territory under their direct administration. Judea was now governed by a series of Roman governors (or procurators), "whose chief responsibility was to collect and deliver an annual tax to the empire," according to author Joseph Telushkin. "Whatever the procurators raised beyond the quota assigned, they could keep. Not surprisingly, they often imposed confiscatory taxes." Even more upsetting to the Jews, Rome took over the appointment of their most important religious leader, the high priest. Consequently, Telushkin observes, the high priests "increasingly came from the ranks of Jews who collaborated with Rome."[3]

Shortly before the Romans placed Judea under their direct administration, Jesus of Nazareth, on whose life and teachings the Christian religion is based, was born in Bethlehem, near Jerusalem. In about A.D. 30, the Roman procurator Pontius Pilate, keenly aware of the increasing dissatisfaction with Roman rule among his Jewish subjects, had Jesus crucified on suspicion of trying to stir up a revolt among his fellow Jews. After Jesus' execution, the Roman government appointed a series of particularly autocratic and brutal procurators to oversee Judea. In response, in A.D. 66, a group of Jewish insurgents called the Zealots rose up against their hated overlords and managed to gain control of Jerusalem. But the Zealots and their supporters proved no match for the greatest military machine on earth, and, four years later, the Roman army retook Jerusalem and burned most of the city's buildings to the ground, including the Second Temple. All that survived of the Temple was one retaining wall on the western side of the building's courtyard. Dubbed the "Western Wall," this last remnant of the Temple remains Judaism's holiest site 2,000 years later.

The Zealot Rebellion proved a disaster for the Jews. Not only was the Second Temple destroyed, but also by the time the last Jewish outpost at Masada had fallen to the Roman army in A.D. 73, as many as one million Jews had been killed and thousands of others sold into slavery by their Roman overlords. In A.D. 132, the Jews made one last attempt to overthrow the Romans in what has come to be known as the Bar-Kokhba

In this bas-relief from the Arch of Titus in Rome, Italy, men are depicted carrying off treasures from the Second Temple in Jerusalem. The Roman army, led by the future Roman emperor Titus, besieged and conquered the city of Jerusalem. The city and its famous temple were destroyed.

Revolt, in honor of its leader, Simeon Bar-Kokhba. When the Romans finally suppressed the rebellion three years later, they made it clear they had no intention of dealing with the troublesome Judeans ever again. "To blot out all Jewish ties with the land, Judea was renamed Syria Palestina [later shortened to Palestina or Palestine] and Jerusalem, Aelia Capitolina," writes historian Bernard Reich.[4] Except for a tiny remnant, the entire Jewish community was exiled by Roman officials. To repopulate and rebuild Jerusalem and the rest of Palestine, the Roman government imported thousands of non-Jews from other parts of their vast empire.

THE JEWISH DIASPORA AND BYZANTINE RULE

Following the failure of the second Jewish rebellion in A.D. 135, most Jews were forced to live outside of their homeland in what is today known as the Jewish Diaspora. (Diaspora comes from an ancient Greek word meaning "scattered" or "dispersed.") The small Jewish minority that remained in Palestine after the revolt was located almost entirely in what is today the northern part of the State of Israel. Jews were strictly barred from entering their holiest city, Jerusalem, except for one day each year—Tisha B'av, which is the ninth of the month of Av in the Hebrew calendar—to mourn for the lost Temple.

In A.D. 395, the enormous Roman Empire was split into eastern and western parts. Palestine fell under the control of the Eastern Roman, or Byzantine, Empire. Just fifteen years earlier, the Roman Empire had officially adopted Christianity as its state religion. During the following century, the majority of Palestine's population, urged on by their new Byzantine overlords, converted from paganism to Christianity. Under Byzantine rule, Jews were still prohibited from residing in Jerusalem, which Christians also claimed as their religion's holiest city, since it was where Jesus was crucified and where they believed he rose from the dead. To further minimize Jewish influence on the religious and cultural life of what was coming to be known as the Holy Land, Byzantine rulers issued a number of other restrictive decrees against Palestine's Jewish community, including prohibitions on commercial exchanges between Christians and Jews and on the construction of new synagogues.

ARAB-MUSLIM CONQUEST

Byzantine rule over Palestine lasted until A.D. 638 when followers of the new monotheistic religion of Islam burst out of the Arabian Peninsula to conquer the region and much of the rest of the Middle East and Spain. With a few brief interruptions, Arab Muslims would control Palestine for the next four centuries.

Muslims believe that the one true religion is Islam. In the early seventh century, when Muhammad ibn Abdallah, a native of Mecca, Arabia, began preaching to his neighbors what would become the fundamental teaching of the new Islamic faith: There was only one God, and his name was Allah. Allah disclosed this great truth to him, Muhammad claimed, through the angel Gabriel. According to Islamic teachings, Allah sent several prophets to Earth to help people understand his true nature. Among them were Abraham, Moses, Jesus, and Allah's final and most important prophet, Muhammad himself. Allah's revelations to Muhammad were recorded in the Muslim faith's holiest book, the Koran, which was written in and, according to Islamic doctrine, should only be read in the prophet's native language of Arabic. Muslims also believe that Islam has five basic "pillars": declaring one's faith in Allah, praying five times daily, donating money to the poor, fasting during the holy month of Ramadan, and making at least one pilgrimage to Mecca.

Under Arab rule, caliphs, who were the customary civil and religious leaders of Islamic states, governed Palestine first from neighboring Syria, then from Iraq, and finally from Egypt. The Arab caliph Ulmar, whose armies first conquered Jerusalem in A.D. 638, declared the city as Islam's third most sacred site. According to Islamic tradition, Muhammad ascended to heaven on the very site of Judaism's holiest place, the Second Temple.

In A.D. 691, Palestine's Arab rulers completed construction of the Dome of the Rock, the spectacular Islamic shrine, on the place where the Temple had once stood. Palestine's Jewish residents were dismayed by the erection of an Islamic shrine on the site of the demolished Temple. Nonetheless, during the first decades of Arab rule, they enjoyed more religious and political freedom than they had under Roman or Byzantine rule. For the first time in five centuries, they were allowed to trade and reside in Jerusalem and worship any time they chose at the Western Wall. However, in common with Palestinian Christians, under Muslim rule Jews were obliged to pay special land and poll taxes in return for governmental protection, "which safeguarded their lives, property, and freedom of worship,"[5] writes historian Reich.

During the early eighth century, A.D., Arab policies toward Jews and Christians in Palestine and the rest of the Middle Eastern territories they controlled became significantly harsher. Most historians attribute this change to the influence of Caliph Omar II (A.D. 717–720), who doubted the loyalty of the religious minorities within his vast empire. Therefore, Christians and Jews were subjected to increased economic, legal, and religious discrimination under Omar II. Burdened with heavier taxes, they were also prohibited from bearing arms and from testifying against Muslims in court. To add insult to injury, they had to ride donkeys instead of horses, cede the road to any Muslims they encountered along their way, and wear distinctive clothing in public. These humiliating and oppressive new policies spurred many people throughout Palestine to convert to Islam. These new conversions, combined with a steady flow of Muslims into Palestine's towns, had changed the region's dominant religion from Christianity to Islam.

CRUSADERS AND MAMLUKS

During the ninth century, the Fatimid dynasty, a Muslim Arab caliphate centered in Egypt, took control of Palestine. By the early eleventh century, however, a power struggle had developed between the Fatimids and their new non–Arab Muslim rivals in the Middle East, the Seljuk Turks. As Fatimid and Seljuk forces fought to control Jerusalem, many of the city's churches were destroyed in the process. At the same time, the warlike Seljuks were also expanding into Anatolia (the Asian area of Turkey), the easternmost part of the Christian Byzantine Empire.

In 1095, Pope Urban II called on Christian Europeans to assist the struggling Byzantine Empire in driving the Seljuk

Turks out of Anatolia. He also asked these Christian Crusaders to take on an even more daunting task. After the men had freed Anatolia from its Turkish invaders, the pope urged the Crusaders to continue southward into Palestine to free Jerusalem and the rest of the Holy Land from Muslim rule.

Fired up by the pope and their Christian kings, the Crusaders arrived at the walls of Jerusalem in June 1099 after pushing the Turks out of Anatolia. Following a five-week siege, the Crusaders captured the city, which had recently reverted back from Seljuk to Fatimid control. Once in control of the Holy City, the Crusaders massacred anyone they considered to be a heathen—Jews as well as Muslims. They also revived the old Byzantine edict forbidding Jews from entering Jerusalem except for the yearly observance of Tisha B'av.

The European Crusaders' rule over the Holy Land was to prove short-lived. In 1187, the celebrated Muslim general and sultan Salah Ad-din Yusuf Ibn Ayyub, better known today as Saladin, crushed the Crusaders in battle and ran them out of Jerusalem. Once the Crusaders departed, Jews, although burdened with the customary high taxes demanded of all non-Muslims, were at least allowed to reside, carry on trade, and worship in Jerusalem again. Now largely restricted to a string of fortified castles and towns along the Mediterranean coast, the Crusaders made several attempts to regain Jerusalem from the Muslims over the course of the next century. In 1291, however, the Europeans were decisively defeated and ousted from Palestine and neighboring Syria by the newest Muslim superpower in the Middle East, the ethnically Turkish Mamluk dynasty of Egypt.

The Mamluk sultans, who ruled their vast Middle Eastern empire from Cairo, viewed Jerusalem as a provincial backwater and largely neglected the city along with the rest of Palestine. Economic decline, linked to the Mamluks' decision to destroy Palestine's seaports in hopes of safeguarding the region against a new crusade as well as any epidemic diseases, also took its toll on the Jewish community and the entire region during the Mamluk era. During the 1500s, the Mamluk dynasty became embroiled in a power struggle with the rising Turkish Ottoman Empire headquartered in Istanbul (formerly Constantinople) for control of the Muslim world. On August 24, 1516, the course of Palestinian—and Middle Eastern—history was changed forever when the Ottoman sultan Selim I decisively defeated Mamluk armies near Aleppo, Syria, and most of western Asia fell under what would turn out to be four centuries of Turkish Ottoman rule.

A Persecuted People

By the time the Turkish Ottoman Empire had conquered Palestine and most of the Middle East in the early 1500s, Jews had been living in Europe as a persecuted minority for several centuries. Following the second Jewish revolt against Rome, some of the Jewish exiles settled elsewhere in Western Asia and North Africa, which already had substantial Jewish communities, and in Yemen on the Arabian Peninsula. But tens of thousands of other Judeans fled the Middle East to the European continent, to begin a new life far from their homeland.

The most important center of European Jewish culture in the early Middle Ages, from about A.D. 400 to 1000, was in Muslim Spain. Under Spain's unusually tolerant Muslim leaders, Jews became prominent in business, trade, science, and medicine and even held high governmental positions following the Islamic conquest of the Iberian Peninsula in the early 700s. In the rest of Western Europe, which was overwhelmingly Christian, Jews were considerably less well accepted. Despite this, many Jews still managed to establish themselves as successful artisans or merchants.

JEWS IN MEDIEVAL AND RENAISSANCE EUROPE

Prejudice against Jews increased dramatically among Europe's Christian majority during the late eleventh century. The inauguration of the Crusades, which sought to wrest the Holy Land from Jews and Muslims alike, was a major factor in the growing anti-Semitic, or anti-Jewish, sentiment. On their way to Palestine to drive the nonbelievers out of the cradle of Christianity, zealous Crusaders left a trail of destruction and death in Jewish villages and towns, particularly along the Rhine and Danube rivers. Adding to the anti-Semitic hysteria was a growing conviction among the general populace (encouraged by some officials in the Catholic Church) that Jewish leaders, and by extension, the Jewish people as a whole, somehow bore responsibility for Jesus' death. The so-called blood libel also developed in Europe around this time. According to this widely circulated myth, Jews kidnapped and murdered innocent Christian children in order to use their blood in secret religious rituals. By the early 1300s, popular hostility against Jews had escalated to the point that the French and English governments, and many central European leaders, expelled them altogether from their countries.

During the mid-fourteenth century, things went from bad to worse for European Jews with the outbreak of the lethal pandemic known as the Black Death. From the late 1340s through the early 1350s, the Black Death killed an estimated 25 to 45 million Europeans—representing from 33 to 60 percent of the continent's total population. The pandemic was likely a combination of bubonic plague and two other less common plague strains. Yet, at the time that it was ravaging Europe, no one had the slightest idea of what really lay behind the deadly scourge. Some Christian Europeans blamed the tragedy on their own sinfulness, viewing the epidemic as a punishment from God for their evil deeds or weak faith. Others, however, were convinced that the "Christ killers" were behind the Black Death. Soon rumors began to spread that the pestilence was rooted in a diabolical Jewish conspiracy to kill off all Christians. Jews, it was said, used black magic to concoct a plague-causing poison, which they then secretly poured into the wells of Christian communities throughout Europe.

At the height of the Black Death pandemic in the late 1340s, angry Christian mobs slaughtered Jews in hundreds of communities in France, Italy, Switzerland, and Germany. The anti-Semitic violence was particularly deadly in Germany. In a single day in 1349 in the German city of Mainz, rioters reportedly massacred 6,000 Jewish men, women, and children. Jews who managed to escape vengeful mobs in Western and Central European countries typically fled eastward to the sparsely populated Kingdom of Poland. Poland's rulers had developed a reputation over the years for being unusually liberal in their policies toward Jews. According to royal statute, Jews residing in Poland and other parts of Eastern Europe were guaranteed broad economic rights and protections, freedom of worship, and substantial self-rule within their own communities.

Throughout the late Middle Ages and the Renaissance (about 1400 to 1600), relatively few Jews chose to return to Western and Central Europe from the east. By the middle of the seventeenth century, however, the region's long tradition of tolerance toward Jews was coming to an end. During the 1640s and 1650s, more than 100,000 Jews in the eastern part of what was then the Polish-Lithuanian Commonwealth (now Ukraine) were slaughtered during an uprising led by a rabidly anti-Jewish Cossack named Bogdan Chmielnicki. In the wake of the massacres, many Jews migrated back west, even though

In this seventeenth-century illustration, children are depicted attacking Jews in the streets during Lent. In the foreground, an elderly man flees before a hail of stones in a town square. Such displays of anti-Semitism were far from uncommon in Europe during this period.

they found themselves forced to live apart from Christians in cramped, walled areas called ghettos in dozens of Western and Central European cities from Rome to Prague.

The returning Jews were not only restricted regarding where they could live. They were also closed out of most professions, with the exception of retail peddling, trading, and money lending. (Jews were expected to act as moneylenders for their Christian neighbors because the Catholic Church prohibited its members from charging one another interest on loans.)

THE RISE OF MODERN ANTI-SEMITISM

By the end of the 1700s, European Jews, encouraged by the ideals of human equality and religious tolerance promoted by Enlightenment thinkers and the French Revolution of 1789, had begun to campaign for "emancipation"—equality under the law and full citizenship. With France leading the way, most Western and Central European states emancipated their Jewish populations during the first half of the 1800s. Old restrictions on employment and residence for Jews were lifted in one country after another and the Jewish populations' fundamental civil and political rights were guaranteed by law. For the first time, Jews were free to enter general universities and move into more prestigious and better-paid professions such as law, medicine, and engineering. Yet, just as it seemed that they were finally on the verge of being fully integrated into European society, Jews found themselves confronting a new kind of prejudice, one based on race and nationalism rather than religion.

The new form of anti-Semitism that developed in Europe during the second half of the 1800s assumed that Jewishness was not simply a matter of following certain religious beliefs and practices. Instead, it insisted that Jews were a separate—and innately inferior—race. The term "anti-Semitism" appeared for the first time in 1879 in a racist tract written by Wilhelm Marr, a German journalist. Marr came up with the idea of describing Jews as Semites after reading a scholarly article on the development of languages, in which Hebrew was described as a Semitic tongue. By labeling his prejudice against Jews as anti-Semitism, Marr meant to emphasize the supposedly scientific basis of his hostility toward their "race." Jewishness was a flaw in the genes, according to Marr, and nothing could be done to correct that flaw. Since Jewishness was of the blood, a Jew would always be a Jew, even after becoming a convert to the Christian religion.

Closely linked to the rise of racial anti-Semitism was the increasing influence of nationalist ideology in nineteenth-century Europe. According to nationalist ideology, a particular nation or people defined themselves by their shared cultural traditions and bloodlines. By this definition, Jews were outsiders in every European nation in which they resided, even if their ancestors had first arrived there centuries earlier. "By the late nineteenth century Jews were painfully realizing that whereas they truly believed that they were loyal and bona fide [genuine] Frenchmen or Germans, many non-Jews did not view them in that way," notes historian Colin Shindler.[1]

THE PLIGHT OF JEWS IN RUSSIA

The growing perception among many Christian Europeans of Jews as untrustworthy alien intruders during the second half of the nineteenth century was particularly strong in czarist Russia, the only major European power that had failed to emancipate its Jewish population during the decades following the French Revolution. In the late 1700s, Poland's neighbors—Russia, Prussia (later the eastern part of the German Empire), and Austria—had taken advantage of the kingdom's military weakness to divide its land among themselves, with Russia receiving the territory where most of Poland's large Jewish population lived. Just as Jews elsewhere in Europe were being emancipated from their ghettos, Russia's autocratic rulers, apparently motivated by fears of competition from Jewish commercial enterprises as well as deep-seated religious prejudice, resolved to prevent the Polish Jews from integrating into Russian society. According to royal decree, Jews were restricted from residing or trading anywhere in Russia, with the exception of a western border region that became known as the Pale of Settlement.

During the 1860s, Russia's new reform-minded czar, Alexander II, relaxed some of the repressive laws governing Jewish life in the empire. For the first time, Jews in certain professions, including merchants, doctors, academics, and some artisans, were permitted to move from the Pale to the Russian interior. This liberalization was quickly reversed after March

1881, however, when Alexander II was murdered, allegedly by bomb-throwing Jewish subversives. (In truth, the man who threw the bomb that killed Alexander, Ignacy Hryniewiecki, was a Catholic of Polish descent, and only one of his seven coconspirators, a young woman named Gesia Gelfman, was a Jew.)

Under the murdered czar's strongly anti-Semitic son, Alexander III, the Russian government passed a series of laws to ensure that interaction between the empire's Christian residents and supposedly untrustworthy Jewish inhabitants was kept to an absolute minimum. Jews, regardless of their profession, were once again prohibited from forming new settlements beyond the boundaries of the Pale, while the Pale's Christian inhabitants were now legally permitted to evict Jews from any villages and towns in which Christians lived. "The reality of Jewish life" in late nineteenth-century Russia, writes Israeli historian Benny Morris, was ". . . one of continuous discrimination and insecurity. . . . Basic freedoms—of movement, place of residence, language, occupation, and worship—were severely curtailed or regulated by the state. The restrictions, including prohibition of land ownership, assured the impoverishment and socioeconomic immobility of most Jews in the Pale."[2]

At the same time that Russian Jews were coping with unprecedented governmental oppression, the unfounded rumors regarding Jewish responsibility for Alexander II's assassination were also making them targets of popular violence. During the years immediately following the czar's murder, a wave of vicious pogroms—organized attacks against a minority group, particularly Jews—swept through the Pale. Mobs looted and burned shops, homes, and synagogues in more than 200 Jewish communities, in some instances leveling entire villages and beating or murdering their inhabitants. "There seemed little doubt that the pogroms were pre-planned and, if not government organized, then at least government inspired," writes historian Leslie Stein.[3] Local authorities typically did nothing to aid the terrorized Jews, and the rioters were only rarely brought to justice.

THE EARLY ZIONIST MOVEMENT

Between 1881 and the outbreak of World War I in 1914, some 2.5 million Jews, more than half of Russia's entire Jewish population, fled the Pale of Settlement, convinced they had no future there. While the vast majority immigrated to the United States, about 25,000, influenced by the budding Zionist movement among European Jews, went to Palestine. In the biblical Promised Land of their Hebrew ancestors, Zionists hoped to establish a Jewish national home where the oppressed Jews of the Diaspora could eventually establish themselves as the majority population. (The Zionist movement derived its name from the Hebrew term "Zion," which originally referred to one of the hills of Jerusalem but eventually came to stand for all of the ancient Kingdom of Israel.)

The hope of returning to Palestine had been part of Jewish tradition and ritual ever since the Romans expelled the Jews from Judea following the rebellion of A.D. 132–135. But modern Zionism, which sought to create an independent Jewish commonwealth as a solution to the Jews' troubled existence, did not appear until the mid-1800s. In 1862, a German Jewish writer named Moses Hess, influenced by the growing nationalistic fervor in Europe, urged the creation of an independent Jewish nation-state in Palestine in his pamphlet "Rome and Jerusalem: The Last Nationality Question." The Jewish "nationality," Hess maintained, was linked "inseparably" with the biblical Holy Land.[4] Hess's pamphlet received very little attention when it first came out. But two decades later, in the wake of the dramatic upsurge in violent attacks on Russian Jews, a new Zionist work by Leon Pinsker, a Jewish Russian doctor, had a far greater impact on Europe's, and especially Russia's, Jewish community.

In his *Auto-Emancipation: A Warning to His Kinsfolk by a Russian Jew*, Pinsker warned that the rise of a highly nationalistic form of anti-Semitism made it imperative for European Jews to

(continues on page 38)

ELIEZER BEN-YEHUDA AND THE REVIVAL OF HEBREW

One of the first Russian Zionists to immigrate to Palestine was Eliezer Ben-Yehuda, known as the father of the modern Hebrew language. Born in Lithuania on January 7, 1858, as Eliezer Yitzhak Perelman, Ben-Yehuda (Hebrew for "son of Judah") became an ardent Zionist as a student in the late 1870s. Around the same time, he also became convinced that in order to build an enduring national homeland in Palestine, the Jews of the Diaspora needed a common language. That shared tongue, Ben-Yehuda believed, should be the ancient language of their Hebrew ancestors, even though Hebrew had not been spoken in everyday life for nearly 20 centuries.

In 1881, Ben-Yehuda left Europe for Jerusalem. Once there, he moved ahead with his plan to bring fresh life to the fossilized language of the ancient scriptures by coining new Hebrew words for commonly used modern terms. Several years later, Ben-Yehuda and several Jewish friends in Jerusalem formed a committee with the declared mission of "spreading the Hebrew language and speech among people in all walks of life."* Under Ben-Yehuda's skillful direction, the committee started compiling a dictionary of ancient and modern Hebrew words and establishing a uniform system of pronunciation. They also urged teachers in Jewish schools in Palestine to use Hebrew as their sole language of instruction.

During the late nineteenth and early twentieth centuries, Ben-Yehuda's efforts to make Hebrew the common

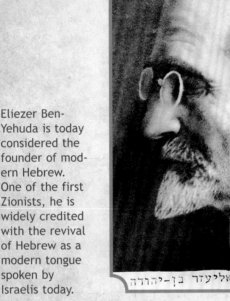

אליעזר בֶּן-יהודה

Eliezer Ben-Yehuda is today considered the founder of modern Hebrew. One of the first Zionists, he is widely credited with the revival of Hebrew as a modern tongue spoken by Israelis today.

spoken language among the Zionist settlers in Palestine were embraced by successive waves of Russian-, German-, and Yiddish-speaking Eastern and Central European immigrants, as well as by Arabic-speaking Jewish immigrants. (Yiddish, derived from the German language, was spoken by many Jews, particularly Eastern Europeans.) Twenty-six years after Ben-Yehuda's death in 1922, Hebrew was declared the official language of the new State of Israel.

* Quoted in Martin Gilbert, *Israel: A History*, New York: William Morrow and Company, 1998, p. 8.

(continued from page 35)

find their national home. Whether that home was located in the historic Kingdom of Israel or in some sparsely populated spot elsewhere on the globe did not matter, he insisted. The then-recent pogroms in Russia had underlined the deeply humiliating and precarious plight of the Jews of the Diaspora, who were "everywhere guests . . . and nowhere at home," Pinsker cautioned his Jewish readers.

> When we are ill-used, robbed, plundered and dishonored we dare not defend ourselves, and, worse still, we take it almost as a matter of course. . . . Though you prove patriots a thousand times . . . some fine morning you find yourselves crossing the border and you are reminded by the mob that you are, after all, nothing but vagrants and parasites, outside the protection of the law.[5]

In the spring of 1881, even before *Auto-Emancipation* first appeared in print, societies dedicated to planning and funding Jewish settlements in Palestine had begun to form in cities and towns throughout the Pale. Within a few years, these societies had united into a loose confederation of Eastern European Zionists called *Hibbat Zion* ("Love of Zion") headed by Leon Pinsker himself. The Bilu, one of the very first of these Russian Zionist groups to be founded, sent 14 pioneers to buy land and establish self-supporting farms in Palestine on June 30, 1882. Although few in number, the Bilu'im forged a path for others to follow.

PALESTINE AT THE START OF THE FIRST ALIYAH

By the end of 1882, several thousand Russian Jews from a variety of Hibbat Zion groups had immigrated to Palestine as part of what would come to be called the First Aliyah. (*Aliyah* is a Hebrew word meaning an "ascension" or wave of immigration to Zion.) When the first Zionists arrived in Palestine,

One of the European nations that suffered from waves of anti-Semitic violence was Russia. In this painting of a Jewish household following a pogrom, a Russian-Jewish soldier returns home to find the bodies of his murdered family. Many millions of Jews fled such violence between the years 1881 and 1914.

approximately half a million people lived in the region, at least 85 percent of whom were Muslim. About 40,000, or less than 10 percent, of Palestine's residents were Christian. (Most of them were Arabs whose ancestors had converted to the Greek Orthodox Church centuries earlier.) An even smaller number, perhaps 20,000 to 25,000, or between 4 and 5 percent of the total population, was Jewish.

Over the centuries, Jews from every corner of the Diaspora had continued to trickle into the Holy Land. The immigrants, including Ashkenazim (European Jews), Sephardim (descendents of Jews who were expelled in mass from Spain and Portugal in the late 1400s), and so-called Oriental Jews from West Asia and North Africa, tended to be deeply religious, and most settled in the holiest Jewish city, Jerusalem. "The small, pre-Zionist Jewish population of Palestine—usually referred to collectively as the Old *Yishuv* (literally, the 'old settlement')—was largely poor," writes historian Morris. "Many if not most lived on charity from their coreligionists [people of the same religion] abroad."[6] Some labored as craftsmen or shopkeepers, but the majority spent their days praying and studying the Hebrew Scriptures. On the whole, the Old Yishuv was disapproving of the new Zionist immigrants, whom they viewed as motivated by worldly concerns instead of spiritual ones in coming to Eretz Israel. They worried that Zionism would forever alter "Judaism by its focus on a political objective, a Jewish state, rather than sustaining a central sense of devotion and Jewish ritual observance,"[7] contends Bernard Reich.

When the First Aliyah began in 1882, the vast majority of Palestine's population was Arab in language and culture—just as had been the case since the early Middle Ages. Palestine had managed to maintain its Arab character despite being conquered by the Turkish Ottoman Empire more than four centuries earlier because very few Turks had chosen to settle in the colony. Administered by Turkish governors headquartered in Damascus, Syria, and Beirut, Lebanon, during the 1880s, Palestine was a neglected backwater of the massive Ottoman Empire, whose Middle Eastern holdings included virtually the entire region except for Egypt and Persia (Iran). Palestine's downtrodden Arab majority, notes historian Stein, "overwhelmingly were subsistence farmers subject to wretched housing and sanitary conditions. Most were illiterate and, plagued by malaria, typhus, typhoid, and cholera, they had very low life expectancies."[8] As the Zionist newcomers would quickly discover, large tracts of Palestine were sandy or swamp-ridden and nearly impossible to cultivate, water supplies were inadequate and often tainted, and transportation and communications systems were shockingly antiquated. In July 1882, the Russian Zionist Leib Bienstock noted in a letter from Palestine that "to this day there are no [paved] roads, not only from village to village but also from the city of one region to another. The road between Jaffa [a major port city on the Mediterranean Sea] and Jerusalem is riddled with ridges and potholes even though the coachmen pay excessive taxes."[9]

SACRIFICES AND TRIALS OF THE FIRST ALIYAH

From 1882 to 1903, an estimated 25,000 European Jews, most of them Russians in their late teens or early twenties, came to Palestine as part of the First Aliyah. During this same period, the new immigrants founded almost two-dozen agricultural settlements, which they hoped would provide Jews with a permanent foothold in their ancient Promised Land. As it turned out, however, most of this first wave of Zionist settlers did not stay. Some returned to Eastern Europe, while others ended up in the United States or Western Europe. Many of the idealistic young pioneers were simply unprepared for the enormous difficulties and dangers awaiting them in Palestine.

Upon arriving in Palestine, most of the early Zionists purchased the only land they could afford for their farms: either swampy tracts that had to be drained before they could be cultivated or arid plots. Few of the Zionists had ever farmed before, and their inexperience combined with the harsh environment took a severe toll on their meager savings and their morale. Only through the generous assistance of a French magnate named Baron Edmond de Rothschild were many early Zionist farming settlements able to survive financially during the first months or even years after they were founded. "Nobody knows of all the hardships, sickness, and wretchedness" he and his fellow Zionists had already faced, Menashe Meyerovitch, a struggling Jewish farmer in western Palestine, wrote in 1885. "No observer from afar can feel what it is like to be without a drop of water for days, to lie for months in cramped tents visited by all sorts of reptiles. . . . No one looking at a completed building realizes the sacrifice put into it."[10]

Those few Zionists who had the financial means to purchase more desirable tracts of farmland in Palestine often found themselves the targets of deep hostility from their Arab neighbors. By the latter half of the nineteenth century, the best farming and grazing land in the Ottoman province was owned by an elite group of wealthy Arab Palestinians, most of whom lived in cities far from their holdings, such as Jerusalem, Beirut, and even Paris. Before selling their properties to the Zionists, these absentee owners had rented them out to local peasants, who grazed their livestock, raised their crops, and built their homes there. Unable to retaliate against their absentee former landlords, some of the displaced Arab peasants took out their anger over losing their houses, fields, and pastures on the new Jewish landowners. Within four years of the start of the First Aliyah, an Arab–Jewish clash over land serious enough to require the intervention of Ottoman troops erupted in the Zionist settlement of Petach Tikva in western Palestine. In March 1886, a raid on the settlement by a group of recently evicted Arab tenants left four Jewish settlers wounded and a fifth settler, an elderly woman, dead of a heart attack.

In the late 1880s, an even more urgent problem for the pioneers of the First Aliyah than skirmishes over land with the local Arab population was the relatively meager interest and support that the Zionist enterprise had received from abroad. Fortunately for the Zionists, they had found by the end of the nineteenth century an extraordinary leader in Theodor Herzl, an Austrian journalist with the vision, media savvy, and organizational skills to secure the international backing their ambitious undertaking required to succeed.

Zionist Dreams

Theodor Herzl led the Zionist movement from 1897 until his death at age 44 years in 1904. Under Herzl's energetic and adept direction, the Zionist enterprise not only gained unprecedented worldwide attention and support, but also developed the organizational and economic tools necessary to turn the dream of a national Jewish homeland into reality.

The Zionist movement's most celebrated and influential leader was born into a middle-class Jewish family in Budapest, Hungary, in 1860. When he was 18, Theodor Herzl moved with his family to Vienna, Austria, where he soon earned a law degree from the University of Vienna. Instead of practicing law, however, Herzl became a playwright, short-story writer, and journalist. In 1891, he moved to Paris to work as a newspaper correspondent for the liberal Vienna periodical *Neue Freie Presse (New Free Press)*.

Herzl had personally experienced anti-Semitism while studying at the University of Vienna and was well aware of the oppressive conditions Jews in Russia faced. Nonetheless, he was shocked by the level of anti-Semitism he encountered in Paris, the birthplace of the egalitarian French Revolution a century earlier. In 1894, Herzl was assigned to cover the heavily publicized treason case of Captain Alfred Dreyfus, the only Jew on the general staff of the French army. Dreyfus was convicted of spying for Germany, France's longtime enemy, and sentenced to life imprisonment even though his prosecutors failed to produce a shred of solid evidence against him. At Dreyfus's humiliating public demotion, Herzl listened in horror as a crowd of onlookers, inflamed by Paris's rabidly anti-Semitic press, chanted "Death to the Jews!"[1] Once, Herzl had believed that it was just a matter of time before Jews were fully assimilated into European society and culture. But the Dreyfus Affair convinced him that Jews were destined to remain distrusted outsiders in their countries of residence forever. Herzl concluded that his people would never be truly safe until they had a nation of their own. (After spending four years in prison, Alfred Dreyfus was pardoned by France's president in 1899. His military rank, however, was not restored until 1906.)

In 1896, Herzl argued his case for the creation of a Jewish commonwealth in *The Jewish State: A Modern Solution of the Jewish Question*, a book that would become the manifesto of the Zionist movement. He told his fellow Jews:

No one can deny the gravity of the situation of the Jews. Wherever they live in perceptible numbers, they are more or less persecuted. . . . Can we hope for better days, . . . can we wait in pious resignation till the princes and peoples of this earth are more mercifully disposed towards us? I say that we cannot hope for a change in the current of feeling. . . . The nations in whose midst Jews live are all either covertly

In this 1897 photo, Theodor Herzl looks out at the Rhine River while stand-ing at the balcony of the hotel in Basel, Switzerland, where he stayed dur-ing the First Zionist Congress. The congress established the World Zionist Organization with the goal of returning Jews to their ancestral homeland in Palestine.

or openly Anti-Semitic. . . . Let the sovereignty be granted us over a portion of the globe large enough to satisfy the rightful requirements of a nation; the rest we shall manage for ourselves.[2]

BUILDING BLOCKS OF ZIONISM

In *The Jewish State*, Herzl stressed that Jews must commit themselves to a more ambitious emigration plan than the

HERZL'S DIPLOMATIC EFFORTS

Theodor Herzl was convinced that diplomacy was the most effective path to realizing the Zionist dream of a Jewish state in Palestine. To that end, following the publication of *The Jewish State* in 1896, Herzl focused much of his time and energy on trying to obtain an official charter for founding a Jewish state in Palestine from the region's Ottoman ruler. He also arranged meetings with a number of other world leaders to discuss the Zionist cause and secure their public approval for the creation of a Jewish state in the historic kingdom of Israel. Among the leaders he met with were Pope Pius X, head of the Roman Catholic Church; Kaiser Wilhelm II of Germany; and King Victor Emmanuel III of Italy. After trying to arrange a meeting for five years with the Ottoman Empire's supreme ruler, Herzl was granted an audience in 1901 with Sultan Abdul Hamid II. The sultan, although willing to allow large-scale Jewish settlement elsewhere in his empire in return for Jewish help in paying off the empire's massive public debt, stubbornly refused to approve the establishment of a Jewish state in Palestine, a land holy to Muslims as well as to Jews.

piecemeal settlement of Palestine by small groups. Instead, their goal should be the immediate return of the Jewish people on a massive scale to their "historic home" from every corner of the Diaspora.[3] Much of the book consisted of practical suggestions regarding how to build a successful Jewish national homeland in Palestine, including detailed discussions about agriculture, industry, labor policies, and public education in the proposed state. In *The Jewish State*, Herzl also emphasized the

By the summer of 1903, Herzl had become deeply discouraged regarding his failed diplomatic efforts with the Ottomans and the European leaders' lack of interest in the Zionist cause. A rash of deadly pogroms that year in Russia that left hundreds of Jews dead or wounded lent an added sense of urgency to the Zionist goal of a Jewish national homeland. Consequently, in August 1903, when the British government offered the Zionists territory in East Africa for a Jewish state, Herzl threw his support behind what came to be known as the Uganda Plan. (The name was inaccurate, as the land in question was not actually in Uganda, but rather in what would soon become the British crown colony of Kenya.) Herzl only looked on the African territory as a temporary refuge for Jews from pogroms and persecution, and he still clung to the hope of someday obtaining Palestine as a permanent national home for his people. Nonetheless, many Zionists, unwilling to settle for anything less than a return to the Holy Land, highly disapproved of his decision to back the Uganda Plan. When Herzl died in 1904, the controversy over Uganda was still going strong. A year after Herzl's death, the Seventh Zionist Congress rejected Britain's offer of territory in Africa.

critical importance of gaining international political support for a Jewish commonwealth within the territory of Palestine. He believed that the Zionists should not only obtain an official charter from the Ottoman Empire to found a Jewish state, but also secure the public support of the leaders of as many of the great European powers as possible.

Following the book's publication, Herzl traveled throughout Europe to secure backing from the Jewish community for his ideas, which were particularly popular in Russia's Pale of Settlement. In August 1897, he organized the First Zionist Congress in Basel, Switzerland, attended by some 250 delegates from two-dozen countries. The congress established the World Zionist Organization, whose central goal was "to create for the Jewish people a home in Palestine secured by public law."[4] On September 3, 1897, shortly after the meeting ended, Herzl wrote optimistically in his diary: "Were I to sum up the Basel Congress in a word . . . it would be this: At Basel I founded the Jewish State. If I said this out loud today, I would be answered by universal laughter. Perhaps in five years and certainly in 50, everyone will know it."[5]

When Herzl died suddenly of heart failure in July 1904, his goal of attaining official backing for a Jewish homeland in Palestine from the Ottoman Empire or any of the other great world powers was still unrealized. Under his inspired leadership, however, Zionism had attracted a much larger and more geographically diverse group of Jewish supporters than ever before. He also established vital economic institutions. The most important of these was the Jewish National Fund (JNF). Set up at the Fifth Zionist Congress in Basel in 1901, the Jewish National Fund proved exceptionally successful in raising money from Jewish donors, wealthy and poor alike, to buy land in Palestine for Jewish settlements. "Within three years of the fund being set up," notes author Martin Gilbert, "enough money had been collected for the first land purchase—Kfar Hittim (Grain Village) in Galilee [in northern Palestine]."[6]

THE SECOND ALIYAH

Between 1904 and 1914, during what would come to be known as the Second Aliyah, Jewish immigration to Palestine reached never-before-seen heights, as some 40,000 immigrants, most of them from Russia and Eastern Europe, arrived in the region. This second major surge of immigration to Palestine was spurred by the unprecedented publicity and financial support Theodor Herzl had helped secure for the Zionist cause, as well as by a series of deadly pogroms in Russia. The pogroms, which erupted in 1903 and again in 1905, were even more devastating than the anti-Jewish attacks of the early 1880s that precipitated the First Aliyah. In the new wave of anti-Semitic rioting, thousands of Jewish homes and shops were burned to the ground and at least 800 Jewish men, women, and children were killed.

Like their predecessors in the First Aliyah, the immigrants of the Second Aliyah were "practical" Zionists. Instead of focusing on winning diplomatic recognition for a Jewish state in Palestine like Herzl and other so-called political Zionists, practical Zionists focused on farming or, as they put it, "redeeming" the land and rebuilding a Jewish community in Eretz Israel.[7] They believed that once a substantial Jewish population was firmly entrenched in Palestine, the Zionist settlers would be more likely to gain acceptance of their claims from the Ottoman Empire and the European powers.

Over the course of the decade-long Second Aliyah, much of the foundation for the establishment of a future Jewish state in Palestine was laid. A thriving Hebrew press emerged and, more and more, Hebrew became the common spoken language of the *Yishuv* (the Jewish community in Palestine). A military tradition was inaugurated with the creation of the *HaShomer* (Hebrew for "the watchmen"), an armed defense force designed to protect Jewish property and settlers from attacks by displaced Arab tenant farmers. In 1909, the first all-Jewish city in Palestine, Tel Aviv ("Spring Hill") was founded along the shores of the Mediterranean on land purchased from the Turks. By the end of the Second Aliyah in 1914, more than 2,000 Jews resided in Tel Aviv. Jewish immigrants had also founded a total of 40 agricultural settlements in Palestine by then, including a number of *kibbutzim,* or collective farms, the most famous invention of the second major wave of Zionist settlers. (Kibbutz means "gathering" in Hebrew.)

In 1909, 12 Russian immigrants founded Deganiah, the first kibbutz, on swampland near the Sea of Galilee. Deganiah's founders, like many of the Second Aliyah migrants, were devoted socialists. (Socialism is a system of social organization in which the control and ownership of all land, capital, and industry is granted to the community as a whole.) In keeping with their socialist ideals, the *kibbutzniks* (members of the kibbutz) shared equally in both the labor and the profits of their new agricultural enterprise. Everything in Deganiah was collectively owned, from houses to farm equipment to livestock and harvests, and every kibbutznik was expected to take a turn tilling the soil, preparing communal meals, and doing all the other tasks necessary to keep the kibbutz running smoothly. All adult residents also served on the kibbutz's general assembly, or ruling body, which approved the collective's yearly budget; formulated general policies for agricultural production, housing, and health; and approved new members.

WORLD WAR I AND THE BALFOUR DECLARATION

Inspired by the Zionist dream and amply financed by the Jewish National Fund, the Yishuv continued to grow right up to the start of World War I in August 1914. The war, which pitted the Central powers (chiefly Germany, Austria-Hungary, and the Ottoman Empire) against the Allied powers (primarily Great Britain, France, Russia, and later the United States), brought an abrupt end to the Second Aliyah by cutting off new Jewish immigration to Palestine. Indeed, Palestine's Jewish population actually declined during the four-year conflict. Leslie Stein explains: "Since almost all Jews who settled in

Palestine retained the citizenship of their countries of origin, Russian-Jewish nationals were deemed to be enemy aliens. . . . In December 1914, 7,000 were summarily expelled followed, during the next year, by another 4,000."[8] For those Jews who stayed behind, as well as for their Arab neighbors, the war years were filled with hardship. Droughts, a devastating locust plague, requisitioning of crops and livestock for the Ottoman army, severely restricted foreign trade, and runaway inflation led to economic decline and chronic food shortages in wartime Palestine. Yet the war years were also a time of hope for Palestine's diverse peoples. Most believed that the victorious Allies would dismantle the Ottoman's vast Middle Eastern empire, bringing independence to the region at long last. Because of promises the British government made separately to the Arab and Jewish leaderships during the war, Arabs and Jews alike optimistically believed that once the Allied armies defeated the Ottomans, their group would be allowed to govern Palestine.

In July 1915, Sir Henry McMahon, the British high commissioner for Egypt—which was then a British protectorate—began corresponding with the prominent Arab leader Hussein ibn Ali regarding the future of the Middle East in the event of an Allied victory. As the sharif of Mecca, the holiest Muslim city, Hussein was one of the most influential Arab religious and political figures of his day. He was also the patriarch of one of the Arabian Peninsula's most powerful and wealthy dynasties, the Hashemites. In a series of 10 letters written in 1915 and 1916, McMahon pledged to Hussein that his government would support an independent Arab kingdom encompassing not only the Arabian Peninsula but much of the Ottoman Empire's other predominantly Arab territories following the war. In return, he wanted the sharif and his Hashemite clan to lead a revolt against the Ottoman sultan. By encouraging an Arab rebellion, the British hoped to weaken their Turkish adversary by forcing the Ottomans to divert manpower and resources to the Middle East from the main theater of war in Europe.

Hussein's chief concern in his correspondence with McMahon was the boundaries of the projected postwar Arab kingdom, which he wanted to be as extensive as possible. In the

THE BALFOUR DECLARATION

This famous letter from the Foreign Secretary Arthur James Balfour of Great Britain to the Jewish financier, politician, and dedicated Zionist Walter Rothschild was published in the *Times* of London less than a week after Rothschild received it:

Foreign Office
November 2nd, 1917

Dear Lord Rothschild:
I have much pleasure in conveying to you, on behalf of His Majesty's Government, the following declaration of sympathy with Jewish Zionist aspirations which has been submitted to, and approved by, the Cabinet:
"His Majesty's Government view with favour the establishment in Palestine of a national home for the Jewish people, and will use their best endeavours to facilitate the achievement of this object, it being clearly understood that nothing shall be done which may preju-dice the civil and religious rights of existing non-Jewish communities in Palestine, or the rights and political status enjoyed by Jews in any other country."
I should be grateful if you would bring this declara-tion to the knowledge of the Zionist Federation.

Yours sincerely,
Arthur James Balfour*

---

* Quoted in Bernard Reich, *A Brief History of Israel*, 2nd ed. New York: Facts On File, 2008, p. 19.

end, however, McMahon convinced Hussein to give up western Syria and what would become the modern-day Lebanon for the intended Arab state—commercially lucrative territories that Britain's close ally France had already demanded for itself in secret wartime negotiations between the two European nations. Hussein also agreed to temporarily turn over the postwar administration of the oil-rich provinces of Basra and Baghdad (most of modern-day Iraq) to Britain. The Holy Land was not explicitly mentioned in the letters between Hussein and McMahon. Still, Hussein later insisted that the high commissioner had led him to believe that Palestine was part of the Ottoman territory assigned to the Arabs, a claim that McMahon denied.

In the autumn of 1917, a year after securing Hashemite support for the Allied war effort against the Ottomans, the British government publicly supported Zionist aspirations in Palestine in what would come to be known as the Balfour Declaration. The Balfour Declaration was a formal letter to prominent British Zionist and banker Walter Rothschild from Foreign Secretary Arthur Balfour proclaiming the British government's support for a Jewish homeland in Palestine.

Historians have advanced different theories regarding why the British government chose to come out in support of the Zionist program in November 1917. Yet most scholars agree that Chaim Weizmann, a Russian-born Jewish chemistry professor in London and leading member of the British branch of the World Zionist Organization, played a central role in securing the Balfour Declaration. Weizmann spent more than two years lobbying Balfour and Prime Minister David Lloyd George to formally endorse Zionist ambitions in the Holy Land. Their willingness to honor his requests, many historians believe, was directly linked to Weizmann's vital scientific contributions to the war effort: He helped develop the chemical acetone, which the Allies heavily relied on in their manufacture of TNT explosives.

Another motivating factor behind the Balfour Declaration seems to have been the foreign secretary's mistaken belief that

פגישת בלפור בתחנת הנסיונות
Balfour reception at the Experiment Station

Seen here, Arthur Balfour (*the tallest figure in the front row*), with Chaim Weizmann (*to Balfour's left*), at a reception for Balfour at the Experiment Station in Palestine. Historians today conclude that Weizmann was the key to securing what has come to be known as the Balfour Declaration.

Jews in Russia and the United States had a great deal of political clout with their governments and thus could help ensure continued support from those countries' leaders for the Allied war cause. The British could not take either American or Russian support for the Allied effort for granted. The United States had been extremely hesitant to enter World War I and had only declared war on Germany six months earlier, in April 1917. In Russia, the Bolshevik Revolution of October 1917 had just brought some of the war's harshest critics, Vladimir Lenin and his Communist supporters into power. The Allies needed all the leverage they could get to ensure further involvement of these two countries. By officially backing Zionist goals in

Palestine, Balfour reportedly told the War Cabinet, "We should be able to carry on extremely useful propaganda both in Russia and America," where "the vast majority of Jews . . . appeared to be favorable to Zionism."9

THE BRITISH MANDATE FOR PALESTINE

By autumn 1918, British forces, with the assistance of their Arab allies, had driven the Ottomans out of the Middle East, ending 400 years of Turkish rule in the region. In October, the Ottoman Empire surrendered to the Allies. The following month, World War I came to an end with the surrender of Germany. In a series of meetings in Paris between January and June 1919, the leaders of the victorious Allies hammered out peace terms for their former enemies. Representatives of the Allied nations of the United States, Great Britain, Italy, and France assumed the lead in redrawing the maps of postwar Europe, Africa, and Western Asia, including Palestine, at the Paris Peace Conference.

An Arab delegation to the Peace Conference, led by Amir Faysal, son of Hussein ibn Ali, tried to persuade Britain to honor High Commissioner McMahon's pledges to the sharif regarding the postwar Middle East in their correspondence of 1915–1916. But with the fighting over, the British government had lost its earlier enthusiasm for the idea of a large, independent Arab state. Both Britain and France had strong economic and strategic interests in the former Ottoman colonies, which their representatives at the Paris Conference now sought to further.

In the end, the peacemakers only agreed to grant total self-rule to the Arabian Peninsula. At the San Remo Conference of the former Allied powers in April 1920, the other predominantly Arab areas within the old Ottoman colonies were placed under British and French mandates at the behest of the two Great Powers' leaders. The Paris peacemakers had come up with the mandate system to help oversee Germany and Ottoman Turkey's former colonies until their inhabitants were judged to be economically, politically, and militarily ready for self-rule. Each of the former imperial territories was to be placed under the supervision of an established power. That nation would ideally act as a disinterested trustee, helping to prepare the onetime colony for full independence.

While the mandate system was supposed to be more enlightened than the old colonial system, critics dismissed it as a convenient justification for the Allies to maintain control over territories they had seized during the war without annexing them outright. In fact, both France and Great Britain were assigned mandates over Middle Eastern territories they had long coveted: in France's case, Syria and Lebanon, and in Great Britain's, the oil-rich provinces of Beirut and Basra (Iraq) and Palestine. Whereas oil had not been discovered in Palestine, the region did have important strategic value for Britain. Controlling Palestine would help the British safeguard a critical route to their highly valuable colony of India: the Suez Canal in neighboring Egypt, which linked the Red Sea to the Mediterranean.

In July 1922, the French and British mandates in the Middle East were formally approved by the newly formed international organization the League of Nations. To the dismay of the Arab Palestinians and the relief of the Zionists, the official League of Nations mandate for Palestine incorporated the objectives of the Balfour Declaration by committing Great Britain to assist in the creation of a Jewish national home within Palestine. The original mandate lumped together what is today the State of Israel and the Palestinian-administered Gaza Strip and West Bank with the entire modern nation of Jordan (then called Transjordan). By 1923, when the mandate for Palestine officially went into effect, however, the British government had decided to split its original territory in two. In the vast arid region east of the river Jordan, the British established the semiautonomous Emirate of Transjordan, headed by Prince Abdullah, a son of Hussein ibn Ali, as a reward for Hashemite support in World War I. To further mollify their former Arab allies, the British assured Abdullah that the Balfour Declaration did not apply to Jordan.

According to the League of Nations' mandate for Palestine, the region's British administrators were to "facilitate" (expedite) Jewish settlement in their proposed national homeland, while at the same time ensuring that the "rights and position of other sections of the population [i.e. the Arab Palestinians] are not prejudiced [imposed on]."[10] What the mandate's authors failed to explain was just how the British would be able to create a Jewish state without affecting the hundreds of thousands of Arabs who resided in Palestine at the end of World War I.

A Divided Land

Encouraged by Great Britain's ongoing commitment to the promises of the Balfour Declaration, Jewish immigrants arrived in three major surges to Palestine between the end of World War I and the late 1930s as part of the Third, Fourth, and Fifth Aliyahs. Of these nearly 350,000 immigrants, about 5 percent were from Yemen, Turkey, or Iran. The remaining 95 percent came from Europe, where anti-Semitism was again on the rise in the 1920s and 1930s.

Each successive wave of European immigrants contributed to the economic, social, political, and cultural vitality of the expanding Yishuv. During the Third Aliyah of 1919 to 1923, some 35,000 Jews, most of them Russians, had settled in Palestine. Young, energetic, and highly committed, these pioneers founded numerous kibbutzim and other agricultural settlements and furnished the labor to construct much-needed roads and housing. Most of the more than 60,000 Jews who came to Palestine between 1924 and 1929 during the Fourth Aliyah were middle-class families seeking to escape worsening economic conditions and escalating religious persecution in Poland. These migrants settled primarily in Jerusalem, Tel Aviv, Haifa, and other cities, where they helped diversify the Yishuv's agricultural-dominated economy by founding manufacturing plants, construction and shipping firms, and dozens of small businesses.

The Fifth Aliyah, lasting from 1929 to the outbreak of World War II in 1939, brought in nearly 250,000 European Jews, including for the first time a large number from Germany, a nation which had fallen under the control of the ruthless anti-Semite Adolf Hitler and his Nazi party in 1933. Many of the German immigrants were highly successful professionals and academics, whose education and expertise greatly enhanced the Yishuv's cultural, economic, and intellectual life.

ORGANIZING THE JEWISH COMMUNITY IN PALESTINE

The British mandate for Palestine gave the country's Arab and Jewish communities nearly complete control over their own internal affairs. By 1930, the Yishuv had established a number of social, economic, political, and military institutions designed to serve as building blocks for future statehood. The most important of these were the *Histadrut*, or General Federation of Labor; two representative assemblies, the *Knesset Israel* and the National Council; the Jewish Agency, the chief executive authority in the Yishuv; and the *Haganah*, a secret paramilitary force.

Established in 1920 by Russian Zionists inspired by the socialist principles of the Second Aliyah, the Histadrut was not a typical labor union. Under the direction of David Ben-Gurion, a Russian immigrant who emerged as the leading figure in the Yishuv in the 1920s, the Histadrut sought to meet the needs of the Yishuv's working class, from health care to housing to banking to vocational training. It also funded and oversaw large-scale construction projects, cooperative-manufacturing enterprises, and agricultural marketing services for the kibbutzim. Additionally, it helped the Yishuv absorb the hundreds of new immigrants who arrived in Palestine each month. By 1930, the Histadrut had grown from about 4,000 members in 1920 to 27,000.

The Knesset Israel and National Council were representative assemblies formed in the late 1920s with the approval of the British mandatory administrators. Their roles were to oversee Jewish communal affairs, including educational, social, and health services. The men and women of the Yishuv chose their representatives in the Knesset by secret ballot. The Knesset in turn selected the members of the National Council, which handled day-to-day affairs in the Yishuv when the Knesset, which convened just once or twice a year, was not in session.

In 1929, a year after the Knesset's establishment, the World Zionist Organization founded the Jewish Agency for Palestine, headquartered in Jerusalem. The following year, British authorities recognized the agency as the official representative of Palestine's Jewish population. Under the adept leadership of Chaim Weizmann and David Ben-Gurion, the agency oversaw the Yishuv's economic development and all matters relating to immigration and settlement. It was also responsible for the Yishuv's relations with the League of Nations and British authorities in London and Palestine and with Arab leaders throughout the Middle East.

During the 1920s and 1930s, the expanding Jewish community in Palestine was also quietly establishing a powerful and, according to the rules of the British mandate, illegal military defense force. The Haganah, the Yishuv's new under-

Seen here, David Ben-Gurion, as president of the Jewish Agency, during the International Zionist Conference in London, England, in August 1945. The agency was responsible for all matters pertaining to Jewish immigration, settlement, and economic development in Palestine.

ground army, replaced the smaller HaShomer organization created during the Second Aliyah. Formed in 1920 to protect the people and property of the Yishuv against an outbreak of anti-Jewish violence by the Arab community that year, the Haganah recruited thousands from all over Palestine to serve in the militia, smuggled and manufactured arms, and oversaw the construction of stockades around agricultural settlements.

ARAB PALESTINIAN DISUNITY AND DISSATISFACTION

Among Palestine's large Arab community, the process of self-organization moved ahead far more slowly than among the Jews during the 1920s and 1930s. From the establishment of the British mandate until the mid-1930s, the Arab Executive, an anti-Zionist coalition of Muslim and Christian Arab Palestinians, was officially in charge of the economic, administrative, and political affairs of the Arab community. The executive's authority and effectiveness, however, were greatly reduced by Britain's unwillingness to recognize it as a legitimate political representative of the Palestinian community.

Britain's reluctance to work with the Arab Executive was rooted in its leadership's refusal to recognize the legitimacy of the mandate treaty, which they claimed robbed Palestine's Arab majority of the right to national self-determination. Also working against the Arab Executive's organization of Palestine's Arab community was the fact that the country's overwhelmingly rural Arab population revolved around local, clan-based groupings. Arab unity was further undercut by the bitter rivalries that divided the handful of elite families who had long dominated the political, social, and economic life of the region's towns, particularly the two leading Arab families of Jerusalem, the Husseinis and the Nashashibis.

While the Jewish community was quietly organizing itself into an effective political and military force, Arabs across Palestine were protesting—sometimes violently—against growing Jewish immigration instead of focusing on constructing the foundations of statehood. In August 1929, particularly violent anti-Zionist protests erupted in Jerusalem following a dispute between Jews and Arabs over access to the Western Wall. After rumors spread through the Muslim community that Jews planned to destroy the Muslim holy sites in the city, angry Arab mobs attacked Jews in the towns of Safed and Hebron. In the notorious Hebron riots of August 23–24, mobs massacred one-tenth of the town's Jewish population—67 men, women, and children. Dozens of other Jews in Hebron escaped death only because sympathetic Arab neighbors hid them in their houses. By the time the weeklong protests in Palestine had ended, 133 Jews had been killed, most of them at the hands of Arabs, and 116 Arabs were also dead, most of them at the hands of British soldiers or the British-controlled Palestine police. In the wake of the bloody uprising, Palestine's British administrators decided the time had come to reassess their policies toward the region's two major population groups.

THE BRITISH RECONSIDER
THEIR POLICIES IN PALESTINE

In September 1929, the British government sent a special com-mission to Palestine to investigate the roots of the deadly August riots and make recommendations regarding how to avoid such violence in the future. The following spring and summer, two reports were issued regarding the commission's findings.

The riots, both investigative reports concluded, stemmed from Arab fears regarding the accelerating pace of Jewish immi-gration and land purchases since the approval of the British mandate in 1922. In Britain's eagerness to aid the Zionists, some 70,000 of whom had arrived in Palestine between 1922 and 1929, British authorities had paid insufficient attention to the concerns of Palestine's Arab community. According to the reports, Arab Palestinians worried that if Jewish immigration

(continues on page 66)

VLADIMIR JABOTINSKY AND THE REVISIONISTS

Although the Yishuv was considerably more unified than the Arab community was in Mandatory Palestine, it was not entirely cohesive. During the 1920s, Revisionist Zionism, led by Vladimir (later Ze'ev) Jabotinsky, contested the policies of David Ben-Gurion and other top Zionist leaders, particularly in regard to relations with Great Britain.

Jabotinsky was born into a middle-class Jewish family in Odessa, Russia, in 1880. As a young man, he worked as a newspaper reporter and studied law in Switzerland and Italy. Following a series of brutal pogroms in Russia in 1903, he joined the Zionist movement. In 1921, he was elected to the Zionist Executive of the World Zionist Congress. Two years later, Jabotinsky resigned his post in protest over Britain's division of their League of Nations mandate for Palestine to create the semiautonomous Arab emirate of Transjordan (modern Jordan). Jabotinsky insisted that all of Mandatory Palestine, including both the eastern and the western banks of the River Jordan, should be set aside for the Jewish national home promised in the Balfour Declaration. Jabotinsky was disgusted with Chaim Weizmann, Ben-Gurion, and the rest of the WZO's leadership for quietly going along with the British government's decision to grant some two-thirds of the mandate's original territory to the new Jordanian state. Benny Morris notes of Jabotinsky: "His Zionism was single-minded, exclusivist, rigid. He once declared: 'There is no justice, no law, and no God in heaven, only a single law which decides and supersedes all—[Jewish] settlement of the land.'"*

In 1925, Jabotinsky and his supporters formed the World Union of Zionist-Revisionists, so named because they wanted to "revise" the British mandate for Palestine to re-include

A fiery orator and an accomplished writer in several languages, Vladimir (later Ze'ev) Jabotinsky was a militant Zionist who formed the first Jewish self-defense unit in Palestine in the 1920s.

Jordan. In opposition to Ben-Gurion and other leading Zionists, Jabotinsky and the Revisionists also called for less socialist economic policies in the Yishuv and a more militant and united response by the Jewish community to Arab rioting. Finally, in light of growing Arab hostility, Jabotinsky believed the Jews would only be able to establish and maintain a viable state in Palestine by force, a view rejected by most of the Yishuv. According to Morris, Jabotinsky bore "no emotional animosity toward Arabs. . . . He understood, as he put it in 1926, that 'the tragedy lies in the fact that there is a collision here between two truths. . . . But our justice is greater,' he concluded." The Arabs' "instinctive patriotism," Jabotinsky once declared, "is just as pure and noble as our own; it cannot be bought, it can only be curbed by . . . *force majeure* [superior force]."**

* Benny Morris, *Righteous Victims: A History of the Zionist-Arab Conflict, 1881–2001*. New York: Alfred A. Knopf, 2001, p. 108.
** Ibid.

(continued from page 63)

and land purchases were allowed to continue at their present rates, the Arabs would eventually become a landless minority in their own country. Many Arabs were also embittered by what they saw as Britain's failure to ensure that "the rights and position of other sections of the population"[1] were not compromised by their commitment to the Zionist cause, as the official League of Nations mandate for Palestine pledged. To rectify this situation, the reports urged, British authorities must place firm restrictions on Jewish immigration to Palestine as well as on future land sales to non-Arabs in the region. On October 21, 1930, the British government officially backed these recommendations in the Passfield White Paper, issued by Colonial Secretary Lord Passfield. ("White papers" were formal declarations of British policy.)

In sharp contrast to the Balfour Declaration, the Passfield White Paper was decidedly pro-Arab in tone. The White Paper's authors asserted that Palestine lacked enough arable land to support both its Arab population and the new immigrants pouring into the region each year from abroad. Therefore, they declared, significant new restrictions would be placed on Jewish immigration to Palestine and Jews would have to secure the permission of mandatory authorities before purchasing tracts of farmland in the future. Furthermore, the White Paper's authors emphasized that Britain's commitment to facilitating "a Jewish national home" in the Holy Land did not mean that His Majesty's government planned to turn all of Palestine into a Jewish state, but merely that it supported the further development of the Jewish community within Palestine.

The publication of the Passfield White Paper created a furor within the Yishuv and the international Zionist movement. Chaim Weizmann and other influential European Zionists urged Prime Minister Ramsay MacDonald to renounce the new policy statement. Caving in to the pressure, MacDonald issued a letter in February 1931 repudiating the recommendations before mandatory authorities had even had a chance to put them into effect. In his letter, MacDonald avowed that the British government "did not prescribe and [does] not contemplate any stoppage or prohibition of Jewish immigration,"[2] nor would it interfere with the ability of Jews to purchase additional land in Palestine. While Zionists rejoiced at the prime minister's change of heart, the Arab Palestinian community looked on MacDonald's rejection of the Passfield White Paper as just another betrayal by British authorities. "Arab expectations for an improvement in their situation were dashed by the MacDonald letter," historian Eugene Rogan notes, "which they called 'the Black Letter' (in contrast to the White Paper)."[3]

THE GREAT ARAB REVOLT AND THE PEEL COMMISSION

Between 1929 and 1931, Jewish immigration to Palestine declined to about 5,000 a year. Following Prime Minister MacDonald's public repudiation of the Passfield White Paper in February 1931, however, it picked up again rapidly. This was especially true beginning in 1933, after Hitler became chancellor of Germany. That year more than 30,000 Jews entered Palestine, followed by 42,000 in 1934 and 62,000 in 1935. From 1922 throughout 1935, Palestine's Jewish population increased from just under 10 percent to 27 percent of the total population. By early 1936, Arab frustration over rising Zionist immigration again erupted into violence in what would come to be known as the Great Arab Revolt.

The uprising began in earnest after the Arab Higher Committee (AHC), a new nationalist organization composed of representatives from the leading Palestinian political parties and factions, demanded immediate Palestinian independence under Arab rule. AHC leaders also called for an open-ended general strike and an economic boycott of Britain and the Yishuv by the entire Arab Palestinian community. The strike and boycott quickly escalated into violence as bands of armed insurgents carried out a series of uncoordinated attacks on Jewish settlers. The Haganah and other Zionist paramilitary groups fought back. By October 1936, the growing bloodshed, which had already claimed the lives of some 150 Arabs, most of them at the hands of British troops, along with appeals by pro-British Arab rulers in Jordan and Iraq, had convinced the AHC leadership to call off the strike. Yet the violence continued unabated, as Arab insurgents increasingly channeled their anger toward the British, on whose support, they believed, the Zionists' continued survival in Palestine depended. Over the next few months, the rebels bombed police stations, sabotaged military installations and railroads, and murdered dozens of British soldiers and civil officials.

To halt the bloodletting, London again sent an investigative commission to Palestine, this one headed by Earl William Robert Peel. In their final report, published in July 1937, Peel and his fellow commissioners were pessimistic regarding the ability of Zionists and Arabs to ever unite peacefully in a single Palestinian state. Consequently, the Peel Report suggested the region be divided into separate Jewish and Arab states based on population. Partition, the commissioners wrote, "seems to offer at least a chance of ultimate peace."[4]

Under this partition plan, Jews would receive a bit less than one-quarter of the entire territory and Arabs most of the remaining three-quarters. Eventually, the Arab part of Palestine was to be fused with Hashemite-ruled Jordan. Although the Jews were to be given less acreage than the Arabs under the Peel plan, they would receive most of Palestine's Mediterranean coastline and some of its most arable farmland in the Galilee and Jezreel Valley. Most of the approximately 300,000 Arabs residing in territories designated for Jewish rule would be transferred, by force if necessary, to those parts of Palestine designed for Arab rule. The much smaller number of Jews residing in territories earmarked for Arab sovereignty—about 1,200 in all—would be transferred to the Jewish part of

Palestine. To protect British strategic interests in the region, the British would administer a zone connecting the Mediterranean port cities of Tel Aviv and Jaffa with Jerusalem. The Peel Report also recommended that the League of Nations guarantee access to the important Jewish, Christian, and Muslim holy sites in Jerusalem and Bethlehem to persons of all faiths.

Although disappointed by the amount of territory allotted to the intended Jewish state, the Jewish Agency accepted the Peel plan as the best offer they were likely to get from the British government. Arab Palestinian leaders, however, rejected it outright. They would not give up any of their national territory to the Zionists, whom they viewed as interlopers. Arab leaders were particularly incensed by the proposed forced transfer of hundreds of thousands of Arab Palestinians living in the Galilee and other areas that had been designated for the Jews.

Anti-British and anti-Jewish violence by Arab militants escalated after the announcement of the Peel partition scheme. In September 1937, Arab insurgents murdered L.Y. Andrews, the district commissioner in Galilee. In response to Andrews's assassination, the British government forcibly disbanded the Arab Higher Committee and cracked down harder than ever on the insurgents. Between 1938 and 1939, they sent 25,000 new soldiers to Palestine, arrested and deported hundreds of nationalist Palestinian leaders, and sentenced more than 100 Arab rebels to death, of whom some three dozen were actually executed. By the beginning of 1939, some 5,000 Arabs had died in the three-year uprising, and the British had exiled, imprisoned, or killed most of the Arab community's nationalist leaders.

Following the German invasion of Czechoslovakia in March 1939, however, the British had a change of heart regarding their treatment of the rebellious Arab Palestinians. The Great Arab Revolt in Palestine had won enormous popular support throughout the Arab Middle East. Some Arab political leaders in neighboring states had even called for a *jihad* ("holy war") against the Yishuv and what they perceived as its British protectors. Now, with World War II looming in Europe, the British government was wary of alienating Arabs throughout

THE PEEL COMMISSION REPORT

On May 18, 1937, the House of Commons announced that a royal commission under the leadership of Lord Peel would be formed to study the causes of the continuing unrest in Palestine. After an extensive tour of Palestine, Peel and the other commissioners published an exhaustive 404-page report in July 1937, in which they recommended ending the British mandate for Palestine and partitioning the country between Jews and Arabs. The following excerpts from the Peel Commission Report summarize what the commissioners believed to be the central advantages of partition for each group:

> The advantages to the Arabs of Partition on the lines we have proposed may be summarized as follows:—
>
> (i) They obtain their national independence and can cooperate on an equal footing with the Arabs of the neighboring countries in the cause of Arab unity and progress.
> (ii) They are finally delivered from the fear of being "swamped" by the Jews and from the possibility of ultimate subjection to Jewish rule.
> (iii) In particular, the final limitation of the Jewish National Home within a fixed frontier and the enactment of a new Mandate for the protection of the Holy Places solemnly guaranteed by the League of Nations removes

the oil-rich and strategically important Middle East with their Palestinian policies. Hence, British leaders shelved all talk of partition completely, and—as they had done eight years earlier with the Passfield White Paper—published a policy statement

all anxiety lest the Holy Places should ever come under Jewish control.

(iv) As a set-off to the loss of territory the Arabs regard as theirs, the Arab State will receive a subvention from the Jewish State. It will also . . . obtain a grant of £2,000,000 from the British Treasury and, if an arrangement can be made for the exchange of land and population, a further grant will be made for the conversion, as far as may prove possible, of uncultivable land in the Arab State into productive land from which the cultivators and the State alike will profit.

The advantages of Partition to the Jews may be summarized as follows:—

(i) Partition secures the establishment of the Jewish National Home and relieves it from the possibility of its being subjected in the future to Arab rule.

(ii) Partition enables the Jews in the fullest sense to call their National Home their own; for it converts it into a Jewish State. Its citizens will be able to admit as many Jews into it as they themselves believe can be absorbed. They will attain the primary objective of Zionism—a Jewish nation, planted in Palestine, giving its nationals the same status in the world as other nations give theirs. They will cease at last to live a "minority life."*

* Quoted in Bernard Reich, ed., *Arab-Israeli Conflict and Conciliation: A Documentary History.* Westport, Conn.: Greenwood Publishing Group, 1995, pp. 51-52.

that took Arab Palestinian complaints and demands seriously, particularly regarding the pace of Zionist immigration. For European Jews, however, Great Britain's sudden reversal of immigration policy for Palestine could not have come at a worse time.

World War II and a New Partition Plan

I n May 1939, two months after Nazi forces invaded Czecho-slovakia, the British government issued a new, pro–Arab white paper designed both to keep anti-British violence from erupting again in Palestine and to keep the Arab Middle East safely neutral in any future war between Great Britain and Germany. Just as the Jewish community was about to face its greatest threat in the form of Adolf Hitler's diabolical "Final Solution" to exterminate European Jews, Britain's new policy statement all but sealed off Palestine to new Zionist immigration.

THE WHITE PAPER OF 1939

According to the White Paper of 1939, a total of just 75,000 additional Jews would be permitted to immigrate to Palestine between 1939 and 1944. From 1944 on, Arab consent would be required for any further Jewish immigration to the country. The White Paper also severely limited new Jewish land purchases in Palestine and repudiated the concept of partitioning the country into Jewish and Arab states. Instead, it called for the establishment of a single independent Palestinian state within 10 years. Since Jewish and Arab representation in the proposed government was to be based on population, Arab control of the reins of power would be guaranteed in the new state. In the meantime, Britain would help develop democratic governmental institutions in Palestine that included Jews and Arabs. If in a decade the country still appeared unready for the responsibilities of full independence, British leaders would reassess the White Paper's time frame for ending the British mandate for Palestine.

The Arab response to the White Paper of 1939 was mixed. Many ordinary Palestinians were encouraged by its pro-Arab stance, even though they were skeptical about London's determination to actually enforce the stringent new immigration policies. Most Arab leaders, however, criticized the White Paper for not going far enough. They demanded a complete halt to all Jewish immigration into Palestine and immediate independence from mandatory rule.

The response of the Yishuv and the international Zionist movement to the White Paper was one of nearly universal condemnation. Zionist leaders denounced Britain's new policies as violating both the Balfour Declaration and the League of Nations mandate for Palestine, which instructed the British government to facilitate the creation of a Jewish national homeland in the Holy Land. They were also appalled by Britain's decision to drastically reduce Jewish immigration to Palestine in the face of extreme and growing anti-Semitism in Germany, Austria, and Nazi-occupied Czechoslovakia. Incensed by what they viewed as Britain's breach of faith with the Jewish people, Zionists vowed to undercut the White Paper's restrictive new immigration rules. Yishuv leaders quietly worked to strengthen the Haganah, the Jewish community's secret paramilitary force, and plotted to sabotage British naval installations to prevent the Royal Navy from intercepting shiploads of Jewish European refugees trying to enter Palestine illegally.

The Haganah was assisted in its efforts to aid illicit Jewish immigrants by a rival militia founded by members of Vladimir Jabotinsky's right-wing Revisionist movement. The small paramilitary group, the *Irgun Zvai Leumi* (which translates as the National Military Organization), or Irgun for short, had broken with the Haganah in 1937 because they believed the Haganah needed to retaliate more forcefully against Arab assaults on Jewish settlers and property. After the publication of the White Paper in May 1939, the Irgun focused on retaliatory attacks on the British mandatory authorities instead of on Arab Palestinians. Over the next several months, Irgun fighters bombed British telephone network junctions and electricity transformers in Jerusalem and Tel Aviv, attacked major railway lines in Palestine, and killed three British police detectives for allegedly torturing one of their commanders.

WORLD WAR II

On September 1, 1939, Nazi forces invaded Poland. Two days later Great Britain and France declared war on Germany, launching World War II. Now that Britain was committed to defeating Hitler, Jewish leaders in Palestine and Europe, including the head of the Jewish Agency, David Ben-Gurion, and the World Zionist Organization president, Chaim Weizmann, put aside their outrage over the White Paper and united behind the British war effort. Until the war's end in 1945, the Haganah provided some 27,000 Jewish fighters to serve with British forces against the Nazis and their allies in Europe and the Middle East. Haganah leaders also persuaded the Irgun to defer its violent campaign against British mandatory officials in Palestine until Hitler was defeated.

One tiny faction within the Irgun known as *Lehi*, an acronym for *Lohamei Herut Yisrael* (which translates as Fighters for the Freedom of Israel), refused to give up the anti-British crusade to unite against Nazism. During the early 1940s, Lehi repeatedly attacked British political and military targets in Palestine—and even tried to convince the anti-Semetic Nazis to aid them in their campaign. In 1942, British police killed Lehi's founder, Avraham Stern, and arrested and imprisoned many of the group's other leaders. Nonetheless, Lehi managed to carry out several terrorist acts in Palestine and elsewhere in the Middle East throughout the remainder of the war, most notably the assassination of Lord Moyne, the British minister for Middle East Affairs, in Cairo, Egypt, in 1944.

Although Haganah and Irgun leaders cooperated with the British during World War II to bring down Nazi Germany and its Axis allies (chiefly Italy and Japan), they also continued to smuggle refugees from Nazi-occupied Europe into Palestine in defiance of British immigration policies. By the time Britain and its major wartime allies, the Soviet Union and the United States, had achieved victory in Europe in May 1945, Haganah, Irgun, and Lehi agents had brought an estimated 20,000 illegal immigrants into Palestine, most of them by sea on rickety steamships.

By early 1942, chilling reports of the Holocaust, which would ultimately claim the lives of an estimated 6 million European Jews, were beginning to seep out of Nazi-occupied Europe. The Zionist movement's quest for a Jewish state in Palestine now took on an added sense of urgency. Wartime conditions made it impossible to convene the World Zionist Congress in Europe; the congress's last annual meeting had been held in late August 1939, right before the Nazi invasion of Poland. An American Emergency Committee of Zionist Affairs was founded in the United States to fill the void. In May 1942, the committee convened an Extraordinary Zionist Conference at the Biltmore Hotel in New York City.

Attended by leading European and American Zionists and several high-ranking members of the Jewish Agency

This photograph of Jews being deported under German guard was taken during the Warsaw Ghetto Uprising, which lasted from January until May 1943. The need for a Jewish state in Palestine seemed more urgent when word of the brutal suppression and mass extermination of European Jews by the Nazis began to trickle out.

in Palestine, including David Ben-Gurion, the conference resulted in a series of resolutions called the Biltmore Program. The Biltmore Program blasted current British immigration policies for the Holy Land as "cruel" and called for the creation of a "Jewish Commonwealth"[1] in Palestine following the war, with the Jewish Agency rather than the British government overseeing immigration and the development of the future state in the meantime.

By the start of 1944, the tide of war had turned in favor of Great Britain and the Allied powers. Even though the fighting dragged on for another year and a half, Zionist and Yishuv leaders began to believe that the Allies would win. In the meantime, the Nazis and their collaborators were continuing to murder millions of European Jews. More infuriated than ever regarding Britain's restrictive immigration policies for Palestine, the Irgun announced on February 1, 1944, that it was resuming

BRITAIN'S HUMAN RIGHTS SCANDAL: THE *EXODUS* AFFAIR

On July 11, 1947, the *Exodus 1947* left Port de Bouc, near Marseille, France, bound for Palestine. On board were 4,515 Jewish men, women, and children, most of whom were survivors of Hitler's extermination camps. All lacked the necessary immigration certificates to enter the country legally. The ramshackle ship, which had originally served as a ferryboat on Maryland's Chesapeake Bay, attracted the notice of the international press when a British naval convoy began following it across the Mediterranean.

On July 18, the world was shocked when Royal Marines, seeking to stop the ship from unloading its illegal human cargo, boarded the *Exodus* about 19 miles (30 kilometers) from the shores of Palestine and began fighting with its unarmed passengers. Three Jews—one crewman and two passengers, including a 16-year-old boy—were shot to death and more than two dozen others seriously wounded. Eventually, the Marines gained control of the damaged *Exodus*, which was towed to the port of Haifa. According to one horrified eyewitness, once there the passengers were dragged from the ship by British soldiers "using rifle butts, hose pipes and tear gas" and herded onto another vessel for deportation its armed struggle against the mandatory government. During 1944 and early 1945, the Irgun carried out numerous bombings of British governmental offices and communications infrastructure in Palestine, including the national broadcasting station at Ramallah. "There is no longer any armistice between the Jewish people and the British Administration . . . which hands our

back to France.* When the ship landed in southern France, however, most of the refugees once again refused to disembark, and French officials, reluctant to embroil their country in Britain's growing humanitarian scandal, refused to make them get off the boats. Unsure of how to respond to what was rapidly becoming a public relations nightmare, British authorities decided to send the former *Exodus* passengers to the port of Hamburg, in Germany's British-occupied zone. From Hamburg, the passengers were transferred, many of them kicking and screaming, to DP (displaced persons) camps in the heart of the former Third Reich.

That Britain should have forced several thousand Holocaust survivors, including many deeply traumatized former concentration camp inmates and scores of orphaned children, to go to Germany of all places, provoked a storm of international protest. Britain's treatment of the *Exodus* refugees was blasted as heartless and its restrictive immigration policies for Palestine as profoundly inhumane in light of the enormous suffering of Europe's Jewish community over the past seven years. Ironically, in the end, the *Exodus* affair proved a great boon to the Zionists by helping win widespread public and diplomatic support for the plight of the Jewish DPs and the eventual founding of the State of Israel in 1948.

* Quoted in Gilbert, *Israel: A History*, p. 145.

brothers over to Hitler," the underground group's new leader, Menachem Begin, asserted. "Our people is at war with this regime—war to the end."[2]

SMUGGLING JEWS INTO PALESTINE

Once the full horror of Hitler's systematic murder of European Jews was fully revealed to the world after the Nazis surrendered to the Allies in May 1945, many in the Yishuv assumed the British government would abandon its stringent wartime immigration policies for Palestine. After all, two-thirds of Europe's Jewish population had been massacred over the past five and a half years, and another nearly 250,000 concentration camp survivors languished in DP (displaced persons) camps in Allied-occupied Italy, Austria, and Germany that were set up by the United Nations, the newly created international organization. Their homes and shops destroyed or confiscated, their loved ones murdered, many of the DPs were unable—or unwilling—to return to their countries of origin. Instead, they dreamed of rebuilding their shattered lives far from Hitler's killing fields in the ancient Promised Land.

Yet, despite an outpouring of international sympathy for Europe's devastated Jewish community, the British government stuck by the recommendations of the White Paper of 1939. Fearful of a violent Arab response in the Middle East—and, perhaps, of losing access to the region's abundant oil supplies—the British refused to reconsider their strict prewar immigration policies for Palestine. Resisting pressure from the U.S. government in early 1946 to allow 100,000 Jewish DPs into Palestine immediately, the royal government announced that immigration quotas for Palestine would be set at just 1,500 per month (18,000 annually).

The Yishuv responded to Britain's continuing immigration restrictions by widening their wartime network of illicit immigration activities. From 1945 until 1948, Palestinian Jews, including many Haganah, Irgun, and Lehi members, as well as a number of sympathetic European and American volunteers, smuggled some 80,000 Holocaust survivors into the Holy Land as part of the so-called *Aliyah Bet* campaign. (*Aliyah Bet* is Hebrew for "Immigration B," the code name used by the Yishuv to refer to illegal immigration into Palestine; *Aliyah Aleph*, or "Immigration A," referred to legal immigration into Palestine.)

Most of the illegal immigrants were transported from southern Europe on small boats or dilapidated steamships to Palestine's Mediterranean shores. The British navy intercepted dozens of the Aliyah Bet vessels at sea or as they reached the Palestine coast. Most passengers were taken to the island of Cyprus and placed in primitive British detention camps, which had been built to house Nazi prisoners of war. The best known of the illegal immigrant ships was the *Exodus 1947*, which left France in July 1947 loaded with more than 4,500 Jews, most of them Nazi death camp survivors. Press reports of Britain's callous treatment of the *Exodus*'s passengers after the Royal Navy intercepted the decrepit ship near the shores of Palestine further inflamed growing international criticism of British policies in Palestine.

THE KING DAVID HOTEL BOMBING

In addition to aiding illegal Jewish refugees, some members of the Yishuv turned to terrorism in an effort to force the British to rescind their restrictive immigration policies and, hopefully, to opt to leave Palestine altogether. In October 1945, the main Jewish underground military organization, the Haganah, decided to cooperate for the first time with its militant offshoots, the Irgun and the Lehi, in attacking the British infrastructure and military and police installations. Over the next months, the three groups bombed British railroad lines, bridges, and army and police stations throughout Palestine. In late June 1946, the British responded to the insurgents' costly sabotage campaign by arresting and jailing thousands of Zionists, confiscating reams of documents from the Jewish Agency, instituting a countrywide curfew, and conducting exhaustive searches for contraband weapons.

On July 22, 1946, Irgun operatives, reportedly with the blessing of the Haganah's top leadership, retaliated against the massive British clampdown by bombing the King David Hotel in Jerusalem, home to the British military command and numerous offices of the mandatory government. According to the Irgun and several eyewitness accounts, a warning call was placed to the hotel switchboard 25 minutes before the explosion, although British authorities denied receiving any advance warning. Whatever the truth of the matter, the King David Hotel was not evacuated on July 22, and 91 people died in the blast, including 17 Jews and 41 Arabs, most of them hotel or government employees.

Most Jewish Palestinians expressed horror over the deadly bombing of the King David Hotel. The Jewish Agency denounced the terrorist attack as a "dastardly crime" carried out by a "gang of desperadoes" and called on the Yishuv "to rise up against these abominable outrages." The Jewish National Council also condemned the bombers, calling them "irresponsible men" who had perpetrated a "loathsome act."[3] Dismayed by the bombing's high civilian death toll and concerned about the negative publicity it could generate for the Zionist movement as a whole, the Haganah sought to distance itself from the Irgun. Consequently, both the Irgun and the Lehi went back to operating independently and frequently in open defiance of the Yishuv's chief paramilitary organization. Despite the disapproval of the Yishuv's mainstream leadership, the Irgun- and Lehi-led terrorist campaign against the British only escalated during the six months following the King David Hotel bombing. By early 1947, there had been so many kidnappings and murders of British soldiers by Jewish militants that British servicemen in Palestine were being housed in fortresslike barracks surrounded by barbed wire.

The aftermath of the July 1946 bombing of the King David Hotel in Jerusalem, which had been the headquarters of the British secretariat and military command, is seen here. The bombing was carried out by the Zionist military group Irgun and resulted in 91 deaths.

Back in Great Britain, the government and the public were becoming increasingly disillusioned with the heavy human and financial costs of maintaining mandatory rule in Palestine. Eugene Rogan notes:

In the aftermath of the Second World War, Britain had neither the resources nor the resolve to remain in Palestine. The differences between Jews and Arabs in Palestine were irreconcilable. If the British made concessions to the Jews, they feared Arabs would start a revolt like that of 1936–1939. If they made concessions to the Arabs, it was now clear what the Jews would be capable of.[4]

UN GENERAL ASSEMBLY RESOLUTION 181

Issued on November 29, 1947, the UN General Assembly Resolution 181 endorsed a two-state plan for the political future of Palestine, which was presented in the majority report of the UNSCOP. The adoption of this report by the UN General Assembly reflected strong international approval—at least outside of the Middle East—for the formation of separate Jewish and Arab states in Palestine. The resolution is excerpted below:

> The General Assembly, . . .
> Considers that the present situation in Palestine is one which is likely to impair the general welfare and friendly relations among nations; . . .
> Recommends to the United Kingdom, as the mandatory Power for Palestine, and to all other Members of the United Nations the adoption and implementation, with regard to the future Government of Palestine, of the Plan of Partition with Economic Union set out below. . . .
>
> PLAN OF PARTITION WITH ECONOMIC UNION
> Part I. Future Constitution and Government of Palestine
> A. TERMINATION OF MANDATE, PARTITION AND INDEPENDENCE
> 1. The Mandate for Palestine shall terminate as soon as possible but in any case not later than 1 August 1948.

Moreover, with British rule coming to an end in India, the glittering jewel of its fading empire, one of Britain's chief reasons for staying in Palestine—the protection of key routes to South Asia—no longer existed.

2. The armed forces of the mandatory Power shall be progressively withdrawn from Palestine, the withdrawal to be completed as soon as possible but in any case not later than 1 August 1948. The mandatory Power shall advise the Commission, as far in advance as possible, of its intention to terminate the mandate and to evacuate each area. The mandatory Power shall use its best endeavours to ensure that an area situated in the territory of the Jewish State, including a seaport and hinterland adequate to provide facilities for a substantial immigration, shall be evacuated at the earliest possible date and in any event not later than 1 February 1948.

3. Independent Arab and Jewish States and the Special International Regime for the City of Jerusalem, set forth in Part III of this Plan, shall come into existence in Palestine two months after the evacuation of the armed forces of the mandatory Power has been completed but in any case not later than 1 October 1948. The boundaries of the Arab State, the Jewish State, and the City of Jerusalem shall be as described in Parts II and III below.

4. The period between the adoption by the General Assembly of its recommendation on the question of Palestine and the establishment of the independence of the Arab and Jewish States shall be a transitional period. . . . During the transitional period no Jew shall be permitted to establish residence in the area of the proposed Arab State, and no Arab shall be permitted to establish residence in the area of the proposed Jewish State. . . .*

* Excerpted from Reich, *Arab-Israeli Conflict and Conciliation*, pp. 62-65.

THE UN PARTITION PLAN

In February 1947, the British government announced its intention to end its Palestine mandate and referred the question of how to resolve competing Arab and Jewish demands for statehood to the United Nations. In May, the UN Special Committee on Palestine (UNSCOP), made up of delegates from 11 nations, was created to propose a plan for Palestine. After a lengthy investigation, the delegates presented majority and minority reports to the UN General Assembly. Both reports agreed that the British mandate should end and that Palestine was ready for complete independence. The minority report, backed by the Iranian, Indian, and Yugoslavian delegates, recommended the creation of a federal state in Palestine made up of two self-governing political entities (Jewish and Arab), tied together by a single, central government with Jewish and Arab representation. The majority report was backed by the rest of the delegates, except for the Australian representative, who abstained from voting for either plan. Convinced that cooperation between Arabs and Jews was impossible, the majority report recommended that Palestine be divided into two sovereign states. The states would be joined in an economic federation but would be completely independent politically. Jerusalem, since it was holy to Jews, Muslims, and Christians alike, was to have the status of an international city under UN jurisdiction.

According to the UNSCOP majority report, the partition of Palestine into two states was to be demographically based. Areas with chiefly Arab populations would generally be given to the Arab state and those with predominantly Jewish populations to the Jewish state. The proposed Arab state encompassed most of what is known today as the West Bank—the large, hilly region of Palestine bordered on the east by the Jordan River. It also included the narrow Gaza Strip along Palestine's southwestern Mediterranean coast, a small part of the arid southern region of Negev, and central and western Galilee in the north of

Palestine. The Jewish state was to encompass most of Palestine's strategic Mediterranean coastline, including Haifa and Tel Aviv; most of the Negev; and eastern Galilee.

Although disappointed that Jerusalem had been excluded from the Jewish state, most Jewish leaders in Palestine and throughout the world strongly favored the majority's two-state plan. Therefore, they were thrilled on November 29, 1947, when the UN General Assembly decided to endorse the two-state plan by a vote of 33 to 13, with 10 countries, including Great Britain, abstaining. David Ben-Gurion declared that the UN Partition Resolution was "the beginning, indeed more than the beginning, of [our] salvation."[5] Little wonder Ben-Gurion and the international Jewish community were so pleased with the UN's recommendations regarding Palestine. In 1947, there were only about 600,000 Jews in Palestine, as opposed to nearly 1.3 million Arabs, and Jews only owned some 7 percent of the country's total land area. Yet the UN had given its stamp of approval to a plan that proposed turning more than half (about 55 percent) of Palestine's land into an independent Jewish state.

While Jews celebrated the UN's resolution, Arab Palestinian leaders were outraged. They did not see why Arab Palestinians should be expected to give up so much as an acre of what they viewed as their country. Convinced UN support for the creation of a Jewish state in Palestine was rooted in European and American regret over their failure to prevent the Holocaust, Arab Palestinians also resented what they saw as the UN delegates' decision to sacrifice Arab rights in order to assuage their own guilt. Refusing to recognize the authority of the United Nations to decide Palestine's future, Arab leaders vowed to oppose partition and the creation of a Jewish state in the Holy Land by any means necessary.

The Birth of the
State of Israel

O n November 30, 1947, the day after the UN resolution to divide Palestine into two states was announced, armed Arab bands attacked several Jewish settlements. That same day Arab gunmen opened fire on a bus en route from Netanya to Jerusalem, killing five Jewish passengers. By the end of 1947, the violence had spread throughout much of the sector allotted by the UN to the Jewish state, an area that was home not only to most of Palestine's 600,000 Jews, but also to some 500,000 of the country's 1.3 million Arabs. The British, unable to control the growing violence and unwilling to use their troops to enforce the UN Partition Resolution, informed the United Nations that they wanted to terminate their mandate and evacuate all British troops and personnel from Palestine on May 15, 1948.

CIVIL WAR ERUPTS

During the six months between the announcement of the UN Partition Resolution in late November 1947 to the end of the British mandate in May 1948, Palestine remained in the grip of an undeclared civil war between the country's rival claimants. Ambushes, sniping, and terrorist acts made up most of the fighting during the winter of 1947–1948, as the Haganah focused on securing the lands allotted to the Jews by the UN Resolution, particularly the major roads tying together their settlements and towns. Fighting was especially intense along the one main road linking the intended Jewish sector with Jerusalem as Arabs tried to impose a blockade on the Holy City's Jewish neighborhoods.

By late 1947, the Yishuv was well prepared to safeguard Jewish territory in Palestine. During the first months of the civil war, as the Haganah concentrated on defending Jewish roads and settlements, the Yishuv's chief military force reorganized itself "from an amateur, territorially based militia into a relatively professional army," according to Benny Morris in *1948: The First Arab-Israeli War*.[1] Between November 1947 and May 1948, the Haganah swelled to some 35,000 men and women, including an elite strike force of 6,000 known as the *Palmah*. During these six months, the Haganah also managed to amass a large secret stockpile of rifles, light machine guns, and grenades. Some of the weapons had been purchased illegally from foreign powers; others had been manufactured in secret Jewish arms factories.

The military capabilities of the Arab Palestinians were well below those of the Yishuv throughout the civil war. In sharp contrast to the Jews, the Arab Palestinians failed to organize an effective national militia. Instead, they depended on dozens of poorly trained and uncoordinated village militias and on numerous armed bands that sprang up more or less spontaneously after November 1947. The single biggest Arab military

Seen here, members of Haganah, the Jewish self-defense force, fasten steel plates onto a truck in Tel Aviv in order to make it bulletproof. This was done as part of the effort to minimize the number of casualties caused by Arab snipers during heavy clashes between Jews and Arabs in the early months of 1948.

force in Palestine during the civil war was the Arab Liberation Army (ALA), made up of between 4,000 and 5,000 troops, about 1,000 of whom were Palestinians and the rest volunteers from neighboring Arab countries. The ALA was created and sponsored by the Arab League. Made up of representatives from Syria, Lebanon, Egypt, Saudi Arabia, Yemen, and Jordan, the Arab League had come out strongly against the UN Partition Plan in late 1947.

Starting in January 1948, ALA fighters began entering Palestine from Syria, Lebanon, and Jordan. Although better organized than any other Arab formation in Palestine, the ALA had communication issues between battalions and most of them ended up operating on their own. Consequently, the Haganah, assisted by some 3,000 Irgun fighters and several hundred Lehi members, was able to successfully fend off a string of ALA assaults on Jewish settlements during the winter and early spring of 1948.

ARAB FLIGHT FROM PALESTINE

By the start of April 1948, the Haganah had begun going on the offensive in their four-month-long conflict with the Arab Palestinians. With the end of the British mandate rapidly approaching, David Ben-Gurion and the rest of the Yishuv leadership were determined to secure and consolidate all the territory allotted to the Jews by the UN partition plan. They feared that once the last British troops left Palestine, the regular armies of the Arab countries bordering Palestine on all sides would immediately launch a full-scale invasion of the Jewish sector.

Equipped with a large cache of arms purchased from Czechoslovakia (in violation of a British ban on importing weapons into Palestine), the Haganah wrested control of dozens of Arab villages and towns within the Jewish sector, as well as the Arab districts of such major cities as Haifa, Jaffa, and Acre. An important consequence of the Jews' new offensive campaign was the mass exodus of some 200,000 Arab Palestinians from the territories designated by the UN for a Jewish state by early May 1948. In recent years, evidence has emerged that Jewish soldiers drove many Arabs from their houses and land at gunpoint. Nonetheless, the majority of Arab Palestinians who abandoned their homes for other designated Arab sectors of Palestine or neighboring Arab countries did so voluntarily, although most assumed they would return once the fighting was over. Fear of violence by Jewish forces was the chief motivating factor behind the Arab refugees' hasty departure, particularly after the highly publicized events that took place in the village of Deir Yassin in early April 1948.

In the predawn hours of April 9, 1948, Irgun and Lehi operatives launched an armed assault on the Arab village of Deir Yassin in what was destined to become the most infamous episode of the civil war. For some time, Arabs had been blockading Jerusalem's large Jewish quarter, home to almost 20 percent of Palestine's Jewish inhabitants. Arab snipers in hillside villages above the main highway into Jerusalem had been firing on Jewish convoys transporting food and other needed supplies to the city's beleaguered Jewish quarter. Located to the west of the city, Deir Yassin was one of the Arab villages that overlooked the main road into Jerusalem. Although the people of Deir Yassin had signed a nonaggression pact with Haganah commanders in Jerusalem, Irgun and Lehi leaders were convinced that the villagers had been harboring snipers. Accounts of what happened on the morning of April 9 vary widely, but in the end, some 120 civilians, including women and children, lay dead, cut down by Irgun and Lehi fighters.

If the massacre at Deir Yassin was designed to terrorize Arabs living in the designated Jewish territories, it was extremely successful. The Jewish Agency, the Yishuv's two chief rabbis, and the Haganah high command all loudly condemned the killings. Nonetheless, when news of the vicious attack on Deir Yassin spread through Palestine's Arab community, the stream of Arab refugees fleeing the Jewish sector "became a flood," observes historian Rogan. Several days after the Deir Yassin tragedy, Arab gunmen retaliated by ambushing a Jewish medical convoy at Mount Scopus near Jerusalem, killing all but 76 of the 112 passengers, most of whom were unarmed doctors or nurses. Reports of the bloodbath at Mount Scopus only added to Arab Palestinian fears. "Palestinian morale had been shattered" by the brutality of the Irgun and Lehi assault on Deir Yassin, observes Rogan, "and the massacre of Jewish civilians at Mount Scopus only heightened fears of further atrocity and Jewish retribution."[2]

THE STATE OF ISRAEL IS DECLARED

On May 14, 1948, a little more than a month after the Deir Yassin and Mount Scopus atrocities and just hours before the British mandate for Palestine was scheduled to end, David Ben-Gurion formally declared the establishment of Medinath Yisrael—the State of Israel—at a hastily arranged ceremony in Tel Aviv. Israel's creation, he avowed, was sanctioned not only by the UN partition recommendations of November 1947, but also by "the self-evident right of the Jewish people to be a nation, like all other nations, in its own sovereign state."[3] By this time, the Haganah had secured virtually all the land allocated to the Jews by the UN and had seized some of the bordering territory assigned to the Arab Palestinians as well. That meant that more than 70 percent of mandatory Palestine was now under the control of the new Israeli state.

Within hours of Ben-Gurion's declaration of Israeli independence, the governments of the United States and the Soviet Union, the two most powerful nations in the postwar world, formally recognized the infant state. They were soon followed by a majority of the United Nations' other members, including all the leading Western countries except for Great Britain, which delayed recognizing the State of Israel until January 30, 1949. Not one of the Arab governments acknowledged

DECLARATION OF THE ESTABLISHMENT OF THE STATE OF ISRAEL

The following are excerpts from the Israeli Declaration of Independence, delivered by David Ben-Gurion at the ceremony in Tel Aviv marking the establishment of the new Jewish state. "After being forcibly exiled" from their Promised Land by the Romans, the Declaration declared, the Jewish people

> never ceased to pray and hope for . . . every successive generation to re-establish themselves in their ancient homeland. In recent decades they returned in their masses. Pioneers . . . and defenders, they made deserts bloom, revived the Hebrew language, built villages and towns, and created a thriving community, controlling its own economy and culture, loving peace but knowing how to defend itself, bringing the blessings of progress to all the country's inhabitants, and aspiring towards independent nationhood. . . . The State of Israel will be open for Jewish immigration and for the Ingathering of the Exiles; it will foster the development of the country for the benefit of all its inhabitants; it will be based on freedom, justice and peace as envisaged by the prophets of Israel; it will ensure complete equality of social and political rights to all its inhabitants irrespective of religion, race or sex; it will guarantee freedom of religion, conscience, language, education and culture; it will safeguard the Holy Places of all religions; and it will be faithful to the principles of the Charter of the United Nations.*

---

* Quoted in Reich, *A Brief History of Israel*, pp. 45–47.

Israel's right to exist. This was hardly surprising, since the Arab League had been declaring for some time that the founding of a Jewish state on any Palestinian territory was unacceptable. For months, the governments of Egypt, Iraq, Lebanon, Jordan, and Syria had vowed to send their regular armies to defend Arab Palestinians from the Zionists once the British army withdrew. On the morning of May 15, they made good on their threat when troops from these five states invaded Israel, signaling the end of the civil war and the beginning of what would come to be generally known as the First Arab-Israeli War.

THE FIRST ARAB-ISRAELI WAR

The First Arab-Israeli War unfolded in three phases, divided by brief UN-sponsored truces. In the first phase, lasting from May 15 to June 11, the Israel Defense Forces, or IDF (formerly the Haganah), fought for the new country's very survival, successfully defending Jewish territory from a series of Arab offensives. On June 11, the UN imposed a cease-fire, giving both the Israelis and their Arab opponents a chance to rearm, reorganize, and plan their next moves. During the second phase of the war, lasting from July 6 to July 19, Israel boldly grabbed the offensive, seizing areas allocated to the Arab state by the UN, including Nazareth in the north and several major towns in central Palestine. Despite these IDF triumphs, Egyptian and Jordanian forces managed to gain control of the entire Negev desert in the south, most of which had been designated for the Jewish state by the UN partition plan.

On July 19, a new UN-sponsored cease-fire, intended to last until armistice agreements could be negotiated, went into effect. Over the next several months, Count Folke Bernadotte of Sweden served as the official UN mediator in the conflict. In September, he suggested a new partition plan that would have given the Negev desert, along with all of the West Bank, to Jordan and would have placed Jerusalem under international supervision. Both the Arab Palestinians and the Israelis

During the First Arab-Israeli War, Arab soldiers sought to wrest Jerusalem from Israeli control but failed. The soldiers came from the armies of Egypt, Iraq, Lebanon, Jordan, and Syria.

immediately rejected the plan, and on September 17, Lehi terrorists assassinated Bernadotte.

One month later, the war entered its third and final phase when the IDF broke the cease-fire, after accusing Egyptian forces of sniping at an Israeli convoy. During this last round of fighting, the IDF pummeled Egyptian forces in the Negev with the goal of reclaiming the entire desert for Israel. After a new cease-fire was declared on January 7, 1949, Egyptian troops withdrew from the Negev. By early March, Israeli troops had successfully occupied the region.

In the meantime, Israeli forces in the north launched a major new offensive in late October 1948 that eventually brought all of Galilee under Jewish control, including the sectors originally assigned to the Arab state by the UN. In December 1948, the Arab Palestinians suffered another demoralizing blow when their supposed ally in the war, King Abdullah of Jordan, annexed the West Bank. By the end of the year, the fighting had petered out, leaving Israel in control of nearly 80 percent of Mandatory Palestine, Jordan in control of the West Bank, Egyptian occupying forces in control of the Gaza Strip, and the Palestinians themselves controlling no territory whatsoever. The holy city of Jerusalem was partitioned, with Jordan controlling the eastern section, including the old walled city and the Western Wall of the destroyed Second Temple, and Israel in control of the western section.

Over the next seven months in 1949, all the Arab nations involved in the war (except for Iraq, which refused to negotiate with Israel) concluded UN-sponsored armistice agreements with the Jewish state: Egypt in February, Lebanon in March, Jordan in April, and Syria in July. The First Arab-Israeli War was over, even though Israel failed to sign permanent peace treaties with any of its opponents because none of the Arab governments were willing to recognize Israel's fundamental right to exist.

Scholars have suggested a number of different reasons for Israel's victory in the First Arab-Israeli War. As Benny Morris points out, the Israeli forces had "home court advantages" over their Egyptian, Lebanese, Iraqi, Syrian, and Jordanian opponents including "internal lines of communication" and "familiarity with the terrain."

Furthermore, he notes, all of the five invading countries had only recently been granted their independence from France or Britain, and as a result most had "new armies with inadequate training and no experience of combat."[4]

In terms of manpower, the Arab invading armies had an advantage over the IDF at the beginning of the war. Even so, the various Arab forces were really little more than token armies, totaling about 80,000 men in all. By the end of the war, the

BUILDING A TECHNOLOGICALLY SUPERIOR AIR FORCE

During the civil war, air operations had little impact on the fighting. The Arab Palestinians had no air wing and the Haganah's small, outdated air fleet was used almost exclusively in resupply and reconnaissance rather than combat missions. During the First Arab-Israeli War, air operations took on more importance with the founding of the Israeli Air Force in May 1948.

After its founding, the Israeli Air Force quickly attracted to its ranks dozens of combat-trained Western European, Canadian, and American volunteer pilots who sympathized with Israel's cause. Even though the infant air force had a wealth of experienced and highly dedicated pilots, however, its tiny fleet of aircraft was far inferior technologically to Egypt's air wing. In 1948, Egypt had the largest and most modern air force of Israel's Arab opponents, including 30 Spitfires, 6 Hawker Hurricanes, and other top-notch British-designed and -manufactured fighter planes.

IDF actually outnumbered its opponents, with a force of nearly 100,000 soldiers. At the start of the IDF offensive in July 1948, the Israelis were better armed than their opponents because of the massive amounts of arms, ammunition, artillery, and tanks they had been able to purchase from Czechoslovakia, using funds donated by sympathetic American Jews. (The United Nations imposed an embargo on selling arms to either side in the Arab-Israeli War in May 1948. Czech leaders chose

During the late spring of 1948, the Israelis scrambled to overcome their air wing's serious technological deficiencies. Following secret arms negotiations between the Israeli and Czech governments, Israeli pilots began training in Czechoslovakia using AVI S-199 fighter planes purchased from that Eastern European country. Czechoslovakia, which had remained under German occupation throughout World War II, was home to several assembly plants the Germans had built there to construct the most up-to-date fighters for their air force, the Luftwaffe. After Czechoslovakia was liberated from Nazi rule in 1945, AVI S-199 aircraft were manufactured using designs for and parts from German Messerschmitt Bf 109 fighter planes that had been confiscated from the former Nazi factories. Relying largely on money brought in by future Israeli prime minister Golda Meir on a whirlwind fundraising tour of the United States, the Israeli Air Force was able to buy 25 AVI S-199s and 62 Supermarine Spitfire LF Mk IXEs from Czechoslovakia in 1948. These two types of military aircraft, based on planes used by World War II German and British fighter aces, respectively, would serve as the backbone of Israel's air force during the first months of the Arab-Israeli War and provide an effective counterbalance to Egypt's fleet of fighter planes.

to ignore the embargo, primarily because their war-ravaged nation was desperately in need of income, but also because, after having suffered six years of Nazi occupation, they sympathized with the plight of the Jews.)

Another factor in Israel's triumph over its five opponents in 1949 was the serious political divisions among the Jewish state's Arab adversaries. The "various countries mistrusted each other and never coordinated their military campaigns," historian Aaron Levin observes. "The Arabs' lack of coordination allowed Israel to fight on one front, stabilize it, and then shift troops elsewhere."[5] "The individual Arab states each had their own national interests—they entered the war as Egyptians, Jordanians, and Syrians rather than as Arabs and they brought their inter-Arab rivalries to the battlefield," Eugene Rogan agrees. "Each Arab country had its own concerns, and none of the Arab states placed great trust in the others."[6] The Arab allies particularly distrusted King Abdullah of Jordan. They suspected—with good reason as it turned out—that his chief purpose in joining the fight against Israel was to annex Arab Palestinian territories for his own state. In the end, he managed to secure all of the West Bank for Jordan. Abdullah was officially the commander in chief of the Arab forces, yet the commanders of the various armies were so wary of the Jordanian king that they refused to consult with him.

For Israel, the First Arab-Israeli War was an impressive achievement. The new state had not only defeated a multinational invading force but had also managed to significantly expand its area beyond the designated UN borders of 1947. Moreover, between the start of the civil war and the end of the First Arab-Israeli War in 1949, some 750,000 Arab Palestinians fled or were expelled from Israel, making Jews a majority in the country and opening up large amounts of new land for Jewish settlements. Still, the costs of the war for the Jewish state were great: 6,000 Israelis, including 2,000 civilians and 4,000 soldiers—fully 1 percent of the population—died in the fighting and tens of thousands of others were wounded.

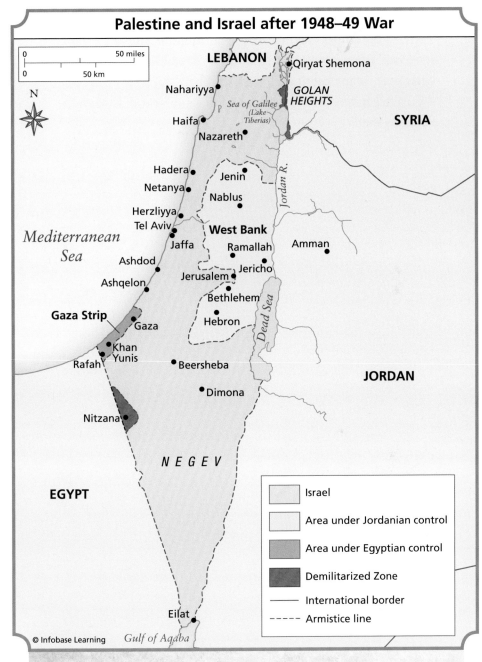

Palestine and Israel after 1948–49 War

0   50 miles

0   50 km

N

LEBANON

Qiryat Shemona

Nahariyya

Sea of Galilee (Lake Tiberias)

GOLAN HEIGHTS

SYRIA

Haifa

Nazareth

Mediterranean Sea

Hadera

Jenin

Netanya

Nablus

Herzliyya

Tel Aviv

West Bank

Jordan R.

Jaffa

Ramallah

Amman

Ashdod

Jerusalem

Jericho

Ashqelon

Bethlehem

Dead Sea

Gaza Strip

Gaza

Hebron

Khan Yunis

Rafah

Beersheba

JORDAN

Dimona

Nitzana

N E G E V

EGYPT

Eilat

© Infobase Learning   *Gulf of Aqaba*

Israel

Area under Jordanian control

Area under Egyptian control

Demilitarized Zone

—— International border

----- Armistice line

This is a map of Palestine and Israel after the 1948–1949 war. Responding to an invasion led by Egyptian and Jordanian forces, Israel seized far more territory than it had held following the UN partition of Palestine. The geographic dynamics established by this war are still largely in effect today.

In addition, many of Israel's best agricultural fields and citrus groves were gravely damaged in the fighting and the infant state was left with a massive military debt. Nor were Israel's trials over. Many more challenges and hardships lay ahead for the Israeli people as they strove to develop and defend their fledgling state.

The State Endures

With the end of the First Arab-Israeli War, Israel's leadership concentrated on developing the political, economic, and social foundations of the young Jewish state. In January 1949, Israeli voters had chosen the first Knesset, the 120-seat parliament, for their new democratic republic. David Ben-Gurion, Israel's provisional prime minister since May 1948, retained his position as the head of the new government. One of the most urgent challenges facing Ben-Gurion and the rest of the Israeli leadership was how to absorb the tidal wave of Jewish immigrants that crashed into the country with the end of British rule.

AN AVALANCHE OF IMMIGRANTS

Almost as soon as the state of Israel was founded in May 1948, the provisional government abolished all of Britain's immigration restrictions for Jews. Within six months, 100,000 Jews had arrived in the country, the majority of them penniless Holocaust survivors. During 1949, an additional 250,000 Jews migrated to Israel.

Feeding, housing, schooling, and finding employment for the hundreds of thousands of immigrants who flooded into Israel added enormously to the economic problems already facing the new state at the end of the costly Arab-Israeli War. Nonetheless, the Israeli government was determined to promote this extraordinary ingathering of Jews from around the globe. A variety of factors influenced Israel's leaders to encour-

THE LAW OF RETURN

Passed by the Knesset on July 5, 1950, the Law of Return legally committed Israel to guarantee full citizenship to almost any applicant of Jewish origin:

1. Every Jew has the right to come to this country as an *oleh* [Jew immigrating to Israel].

2. (a) *Aliyah* [immigration of Jews to Israel] shall be by *oleh*'s visa.

   (b) An *oleh*'s visa shall be granted to every Jew who has expressed his desire to settle in Israel, unless the Minister of Immigration is satisfied that the applicant

   > (1) is engaged in an activity directed against the Jewish people; or

   > (2) is likely to endanger public health or the security of the State.

3. (a) A Jew who has come to Israel and subsequent to his arrival has expressed his desire to settle in

age Jewish immigration on a massive scale. Aside from a fervent commitment to the Zionist goal of making the Holy Land a refuge for persecuted Jews around the globe, they were also motivated by urgent national security concerns. Surrounded on every side by hostile Arab neighbors, the tiny state desperately needed new recruits to build up the national army and to help found towns and agricultural settlements in thinly populated frontier regions.

One of the first pieces of legislation passed by the newly formed Knesset was the Law of Return, which guaranteed Israeli citizenship to virtually every Jewish immigrant to Israel.

Israel may, while still in Israel, receive an *oleh*'s certificate.

(b) The restrictions specified in section 2(b) shall apply also to the grant of an *oleh*'s certificate, but a person shall not be regarded as endangering public health on account of an illness contracted after his arrival in Israel.

4. Every Jew who has immigrated into this country before the coming into force of this Law, and every Jew who was born in this country, whether before or after the coming into force of this Law, shall be deemed to be a person who has come to this country as an *oleh* under this Law.

5. The Minister of Immigration is charged with the implementation of this Law and may make regulations as to any matter relating to such implementation and also as to the grant of *oleh*'s visas and *oleh*'s certificates to minors up to the age of 18 years.*

* Quoted in Reich, *A Brief History of Israel*, p. 59.

This picture, taken in May 1948, shows jubilant Jewish immigrants arriving in the Holy Land a few days after the proclamation of the State of Israel. Israel has come far since its establishment more than 60 years ago but remains mired in a seemingly intractable conflict with Palestinians, who are still seeking their own state.

By the end of 1951, nearly 700,000 Jews—including some 300,000 refugees from Arab countries such as Libya, Yemen, and Iraq—had settled in the fledgling state. Donations from Jewish communities in America and Europe, financial aid from the U.S. government, and German reparation payments for Nazi confiscation of Jewish property helped the Israeli government fund sweeping economic and social development programs designed to facilitate the absorption of this avalanche of immigrants. By the mid-1960s, almost 3 million people lived in Israel, approximately 88 percent of them Jewish and just over 10 percent of them Arab.

CONTINUING ARAB-ISRAELI CONFLICT

Since the day of its establishment, Israel has been mired in a series of violent conflicts with the Arab Palestinians who fled their homeland in the late 1940s and their descendants, along with most of the Jewish state's Arab neighbors. Between 1956 and 2006, Israel successfully defended itself in a half-dozen wars involving the armed forces of bordering Arab countries. The second of these international conflicts, the Six-Day War of June 1967, ended in a stunning victory for the tiny state, leaving Israel in control of the Jordanian-administered West Bank, including East Jerusalem; the Gaza Strip; the Egyptian Sinai Peninsula; and the Syrian Golan Heights. The Israelis immediately announced the annexation of East Jerusalem and proclaimed a unified Jerusalem as their state's eternal capital—a capital not recognized by most of the international community, which houses its foreign embassies in Tel Aviv. The Israeli government further angered the Arab world by insisting the IDF would continue to occupy the rest of the conquered territories until Israel's Arab neighbors officially recognized the right of the Jewish state to exist, something no Arab leader was willing to do. Palestinian–Israeli tensions were also exacerbated by the Six-Day War, as the one million Arab Palestinian refugees who resided in the West Bank and the Gaza Strip now found themselves under military occupation by the very people they believed had usurped their homeland two decades earlier.

In 1978, three decades after Israel's establishment, the U.S.-sponsored Camp David Accords between Egypt and Israel finally resulted in the first peace treaty between Jews and Arabs and the return of the Sinai to Egypt. Following a violent intifada (uprising) in Gaza and the West Bank against the continuing Israeli occupation, the first formal Israeli–Arab Palestinian negotiations began in the early 1990s, when Israeli leaders agreed to meet with the leadership of the Palestinian Liberation Organization (PLO), a confederation of nationalist groups. The negotiations led to an historic two-state plan to

Israel Following the 1967 War

Legend:
- Israel
- Occupied territory
- International boundaries
- ----- Armistice line

Mediterranean Sea

Qiryat Shemona
Damascus
LEBANON
GOLAN HEIGHTS
Nahariya
SYRIA
Haifa
Sea of Galilee (Lake Tiberias)
Nazareth
Hadera
Jenin
1967 Cease Fire Line
Netanya
Nablus
Herzliyya
Tel Aviv–Jaffa
West Bank
Ramallah
Ashdod
Amman
Jerusalem
Jericho
Ashqelon
Bethlehem
Gaza Strip
Gaza
Hebron
Dead Sea
Port Said
1950 Armistice Line
Rafah
Beersheba
1949 Armistice Line
Dimona
Nitzana
1949 Armistice Line
Suez Canal
Great Bitter Lake
EGYPT
JORDAN
Cairo
Suez
SINAI PENINSULA
Eilat
Aqaba
N
Gulf of Suez
Gulf of Aqaba
SAUDI ARABIA
0   50 miles
0   50 km
Sharm el-Sheikh
Red Sea
© Infobase Learning

This is a map of Israel and the territory it held immediately following the Arab-Israeli War of 1967, also called the Six-Day War. Anticipating an attack made obvious by Egyptian troop movements on the other side of the border, the Israeli military struck first, rapidly seizing the Sinai Peninsula, the Gaza Strip, the West Bank, and the Golan Heights.

gradually extend self-government to the occupied territories' Palestinian majority.

By the first decade of the twenty-first century, however, the Israeli–Palestinian peace process had stalled over the key issues of which group would control East Jerusalem and the return of the millions of Arab Palestinian refugees and their descendants living outside Israel. (Israelis have consistently refused to allow the right of return since 1948.) Following the eruption of a second intifada in the occupied territories and a spate of bloody suicide attacks in Israeli cities, Israel began constructing a security barrier in the West Bank in 2002. While highly controversial, the barrier has proven remarkably effective in reducing terrorist attacks inside the Jewish state. Three years later, Israel moved to revive the stalled peace process by withdrawing all occupying forces and Jewish settlers from the Gaza Strip and from parts of the West Bank.

As of this writing, however, a final agreement between the Palestinians and Israelis has yet to be signed, and Palestinians still lack a country of their own. Relations between Israel and Gaza have been particularly tense ever since Hamas, an anti-Israel Islamic organization, seized control of the region from the more moderate Fatah faction of the PLO in 2007. In late 2008, Israel responded to a series of Hamas rocket attacks on its border towns by launching a devastating three-week campaign of ground incursions and air strikes. Israel continues to block all exports from Gaza and tightly controls the movement of people in and out of the Palestinian territory.

In late 2010, President Barack Obama of the United States attempted to revive direct peace talks between the Israeli government and the Palestinians, who are represented by Mahmoud Abbas, the head of the Fatah faction and chairman of the PLO since 2004. But Abbas and the current Israeli prime minister Benjamin Netanyahu remain divided over many issues. The most significant of these are the status of East Jerusalem, how much of the West Bank should fall under Palestinian rule (Netanyahu wants to retain control of the major Israeli settlements built there since 1967), and the right of return to Israel for millions of Palestinian refugees.

Israel's relations with its neighbors in the Middle East also remain deeply strained. To date, the Jewish state has only signed peace treaties with two of the four Arab states that border it—Egypt and Jordan—and its relations with those two countries remain cool. Yet perhaps the greatest threat to Israeli security is the Islamic Republic of Iran, a rising, non-Arab power. Under the anti-Israel leadership of President Mahmoud Ahmadinejad, Iran has provided vital support to Hamas militants in Gaza and to another radical Islamic group bent on Israel's destruction, Hezbollah, which operates out of southern Lebanon. The Iranian government has repeatedly proclaimed the destruction of the Jewish state as a foreign policy priority, a threat made far more ominous by the country's apparent determination to construct a nuclear bomb.

Since the end of the First Arab-Israeli War in 1949, the population of Israel has grown tenfold, to 7 million people, 76 percent of whom are Jews, with most of the remaining 24 percent Muslims of Arab descent. Economically, educationally, militarily, and technically, Israel is the most advanced state in the Middle East, with a particularly impressive record in developing cutting-edge computer and water resource technology. A little more than six decades after Israel's establishment, Israelis can point with pride at their young nation's many achievements. Nonetheless, they realize that their country's continued survival in a hostile environment in which not a single Middle Eastern country has formally acknowledged Israel's right to exist can hardly be taken for granted. Whether the Jewish state will ever forge a lasting peace with its Arab neighbors or the millions of Palestinians who continue to view all of Israel as their rightful homeland still remains to be seen.

CHRONOLOGY

B.C.

c. 1800   Hebrews first settle in what will become the Kingdom of Israel.

931   Kingdom of Israel divides into Israel (North) and Judah (South).

722   Northern Kingdom of Israel destroyed by Assyrian invaders.

587-332   Judah (Judea) overrun by series of conquerors.

142   Hasmonean rebellion ushers in period of independence for Judea.

63   Judea conquered by Romans, who eventually rename it Palestine.

A.D.

135   Romans exile most Jews from Palestine following Second Jewish revolt.

638   Muslim armies from the Arabian Peninsula conquer Palestine.

1517   Palestine becomes part of the Turkish Ottoman Empire.

1882   First Aliyah starts, bringing first influx of Zionist settlers to Palestine.

1896   Theodor Herzl publishes *The Jewish State*, calling for a Jewish homeland.

1897   First Zionist Congress meets in Basel and founds World Zionist Organization.

1904-1914   Second Aliyah occurs.

1914–1918	World War I is fought in Europe.
1917	Britain's Balfour Declaration supports Jewish homeland in Palestine.
1922	British mandate over Palestine begins.
1929	Violent anti-Jewish riots erupt in Palestine.
1936–1939	Arab militants lead anti-Jewish revolt.
1937	British Peel Commission urges partition of Palestine into Arab and Jewish states.
1939	Britain reduces Jewish immigration to Palestine.
1939–1945	World War II is fought; the Holocaust claims the lives of 6 million European Jews.

TIMELINE

1882
First Aliyah starts, bringing first influx of Zionist settlers to Palestine.

1917
Britain's Balfour Declaration supports Jewish homeland in Palestine.

1882

1922

1896
Theodor Herzl publishes *The Jewish State*, calling for a Jewish homeland.

1897
First Zionist Congress meets in Basel and founds World Zionist Organization.

1922
British mandate over Palestine begins.

1904–1914
Second Aliyah occurs.

1947   The United Nations backs plan to establish separate Jewish and Arab states in Palestine.

1948   The State of Israel is established on May 14 as the British mandate ends.

1948-1949   The First Arab-Israeli War is fought.

1937
British Peel Commission urges partition of Palestine into Arab and Jewish states.

1939-1945
World War II is fought; the Holocaust claims the lives of 6 million European Jews.

1937

1949

1947
The United Nations backs plan to establish separate Jewish and Arab states in Palestine.

1948
The State of Israel is established on May 14 as the British mandate ends.

1948-1949
The First Arab-Israeli War is fought.

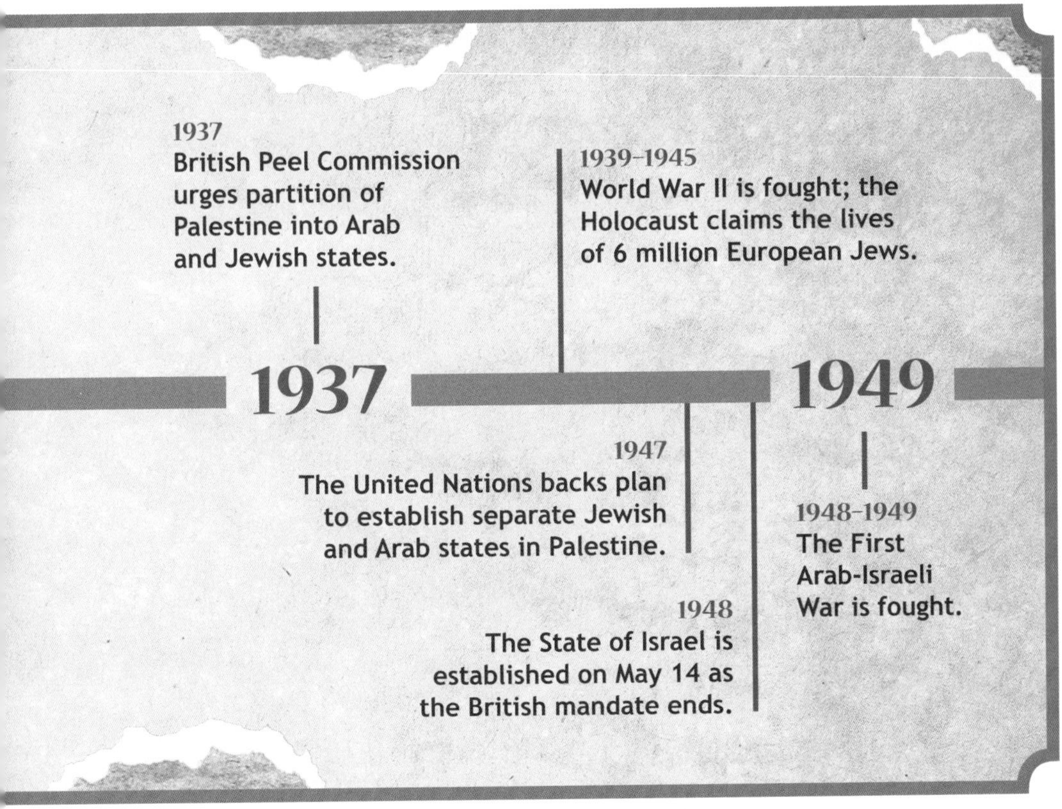

NOTES

CHAPTER 1

1. Quoted in Martin Gilbert, *Israel: A History*. New York: William Morrow and Company, 1998, p. 7.
2. Quoted in Bernard Reich, *A Brief History of Israel*, 2nd ed. New York: Facts On File, 2008, pp. 45–47.
3. Quoted in Gilbert, *Israel: A History*, p. 188.
4. Quoted in Benny Morris, *1948: The First Arab-Israeli War*. New Haven: Yale University Press, 2008, p. 178.
5. Ibid., p. 179.

CHAPTER 2

1. Genesis 17:8 (New American Standard Bible).
2. Exodus 20:2–3 (New American Standard Bible).
3. Rabbi Joseph Telushkin, *Jewish Literacy: The Most Important Things to Know About the Jewish Religion, Its People, and Its History*. New York: William Morrow and Company, 1991, p. 130.
4. Reich, *A Brief History of Israel*, p. 7.
5. Ibid., p. 10.

CHAPTER 3

1. Colin Shindler, *A History of Modern Israel*. Cambridge, U.K.: Cambridge University Press, 2008, p. 11.
2. Benny Morris, *Righteous Victims: A History of the Zionist-Arab Conflict, 1881–2001*. New York: Alfred A. Knopf, 2001, p. 14.
3. Leslie Stein, *The Making of Modern Israel, 1948–1967*. Cambridge, U.K.: Polity Press, 2009, p. 2.
4. Quoted in Gilbert, *Israel: A History*, p. 4.
5. Quoted in Morris, *Righteous Victims*, pp. 16–17.
6. Morris, *Righteous Victims*, p. 5.
7. Reich, *A Brief History of Israel*, p. 17.
8. Stein, *The Making of Modern Israel*, p. 2.
9. Quoted in Stein, *The Making of Modern Israel*, p. 2.
10. Quoted in Morris, *Righteous Victims*, p. 19.

CHAPTER 4

1. Quoted in Rich Cohen, *Israel Is Real: An Obsessive Quest to Understand the Jewish Nation and Its History*. New York: Farrar, Straus and Giroux, 2009, p. 146.
2. Quoted in Bernard Reich, ed., *Arab-Israeli Conflict and Conciliation: A Documentary History*. Westport, Conn.: Greenwood Publishing Group, 1995, pp. 18–19.
3. Quoted in Gilbert, *Israel: A History*, p. 11.
4. Quoted in Stein, *The Making of Modern Israel*, p. 3.
5. Quoted in Reich, *A Brief History of Israel*, p. 16.
6. Gilbert, *Israel: A History*, p. 19.

7. Ibid., p. 13.

8. Stein, *The Making of Modern Israel*, p. 7.

9. Quoted in Eugene Rogan, *The Arabs: A History*. New York: Basic Books, 2009, p. 154.

10. Quoted in Gudrun Krämer, *A History of Palestine: From the Ottoman Conquest to the Founding of the State of Israel*. Princeton, N.J.: Princeton University Press, 2008, p. 170.

CHAPTER 5

1. Quoted in Krämer, *A History of Palestine*, p. 170.

2. Quoted in Rogan, *The Arabs: A History*, p. 199.

3. Rogan, *The Arabs: A History*, p. 199.

4. Quoted in Reich, *Arab-Israeli Conflict and Conciliation*, p. 51.

CHAPTER 6

1. Quoted in Morris, *Righteous Victims*, p. 168.

2. Quoted in Rogan, *The Arabs: A History*, p. 247.

3. Quoted in Gilbert, *Israel: A History*, p. 135.

4. Rogan, *The Arabs: A History*, pp. 250–251.

5. Quoted in Morris, *1948: The First Arab-Israeli War*, p. 50.

CHAPTER 7

1. Morris, *1948: The First Arab-Israeli War*, p. 86.

2. Rogan, *The Arabs: A History*, p. 260.

3. Paul Mendes-Flohr and Jehuda Reinharz, eds. *The Jew in the Modern World: A Documentary History*. Oxford, U.K.: Oxford University Press, 1995, p. 629.

4. Morris, *1948: The First Arab-Israeli War*, p. 401.

5. Aaron Levin, *Testament: At the Creation of the State of Israel*. New York: Artisan, 1998, pp. 17–18.

6. Rogan, *The Arabs: A History*, p. 263.

BIBLIOGRAPHY

Barnavi, Eli, ed. *A Historical Atlas of the Jewish People: From the Time of the Patriarchs to the Present.* New York: Schocken Books, 1992.

Bregman, Ahron. *A History of Israel.* New York: Palgrave Macmillan, 2003.

Cohen, Rich. *Israel Is Real: An Obsessive Quest to Understand the Jewish Nation and Its History.* New York: Farrar, Straus and Giroux, 2009.

Congressional Quarterly. *The Middle East,* 11th ed. Washington, D.C.: CQ Press, 2007.

Gilbert, Martin. *Israel: A History.* New York: William Morrow and Company, 1998.

Krämer, Gudrun. *A History of Palestine: From the Ottoman Conquest to the Founding of the State of Israel.* Princeton, N.J.: Princeton University Press, 2008.

Levin, Aaron. *Testament: At the Creation of the State of Israel.* New York: Artisan, 1998.

Mendes-Flohr, Paul, and Jehuda Reinharz, eds. *The Jew in the Modern World: A Documentary History.* Oxford, U.K.: Oxford University Press, 1995.

Morris, Benny. *1948: The First Arab-Israeli War.* New Haven: Yale University Press, 2008.

———. *Righteous Victims: A History of the Zionist-Arab Conflict, 1881–2001.* New York: Alfred A. Knopf, 2001.

Reich, Bernard. *A Brief History of Israel,* 2nd ed. New York: Facts On File, 2008.

———. *Arab-Israeli Conflict and Conciliation: A Documentary History.* Westport, Conn.: Greenwood Publishing Group, 1995.

Rogan, Eugene. *The Arabs: A History*. New York: Basic Books, 2009.

Shindler, Colin. *A History of Modern Israel*. Cambridge, U.K.: Cambridge University Press, 2008.

Stein, Leslie. *The Making of Modern Israel, 1948–1967*. Cambridge, U.K.: Polity Press, 2009.

Telushkin, Rabbi Joseph. *Jewish Literacy: The Most Important Things to Know About the Jewish Religion, Its People, and Its History*. New York: William Morrow and Company, 2008.

FURTHER RESOURCES

BOOKS

Altman, Linda Jacobs. *The Creation of Israel*. San Diego: Lucent Books, 1998.

Bard, Mitchell, ed. *The Founding of the State of Israel*. San Diego: Greenhaven Press, 2003.

Greenfeld, Howard. *A Promise Fulfilled: Theodor Herzl, Chaim Weizmann, David Ben-Gurion, and the Creation of the State of Israel*. New York: Greenwillow Books, 2005.

Gross, David C. *Israel: An Illustrated History*. New York: Hippocrene Books, 2000.

Slavicek, Louise Chipley. *Israel*, 2nd ed. New York: Chelsea House, 2009.

Wolfman, Marv, et al. *Homeland: The Illustrated History of the State of Israel*. Skokie, Ill.: Nachshon Press, 2007.

WEB SITES

The Establishment of the State of Israel
http://www.jewishvirtuallibrary.org/jsource/History/dectoc .html

History: The State of Israel
http://www.mfa.gov.il/MFA/Facts+About+Israel/History/ HISTORY-+The+State+of+Israel.htm

The Recognition of the State of Israel
http://www.trumanlibrary.org/whistlestop/study_collections/ israel/large/index.php

PICTURE CREDITS

INDEX

ABOUT THE AUTHOR

LOUISE CHIPLEY SLAVICEK received her master's degree in American history from the University of Connecticut. She is the author of numerous articles on American and world history for scholarly journals and young people's magazines, including *Cobblestone, Calliope,* and *Highlights for Children.* She has written more than 30 books for young people, including *Women of the American Revolution, The Great Wall of China, Carlos Santana, The Treaty of Versailles,* and *Paul Robeson.* She lives in central Ohio with her husband, Jim, a research biologist.